ALL YOU NEED TO KNOW ABOUT COMMERCIAL AWARENESS

Christopher Stoakes

CHRISTOPHER
ΧΦΣ
STOAKES LTD

British library cataloguing-in-publication data

A catalogue record for this book is available from the British Library.

Published by: Christopher Stoakes Ltd
                Icknield Court, Back Street, Wendover HP22 6EB

Distributed by: Kaplan Publishing Ltd
                179 - 191 Borough High Street, London, SE1 1HR

ISBN: 978-0-9574946-7-1

This edition published 2019. Printed and bound in Great Britain.

Written, researched and edited by Christopher Stoakes and Viola Joseph at Mews Studio, Bzw and the Chocolate Factory.

© Christopher Stoakes 2019

The moral right of Christopher Stoakes to be identified as the author of this work has been asserted in accordance with the Copyright, Designs and Patents Act 1988.

The Greek script CSL logo ΧΦΣ is a trade mark of Christopher Stoakes Ltd.

All rights reserved. No part of this publication may be reproduced, stored in a retrieval system or transmitted, in any form or by any means, electronic, mechanical, photocopying, recording or otherwise, without the prior written permission of Christopher Stoakes Ltd. This book is sold subject to the condition that it shall not, by way of trade or otherwise, be lent, resold, hired out or otherwise circulated in any form of binding or cover than that in which it is published without the publisher's prior written consent.

This book is a simple and concise guide to a complex, multifaceted subject that is changing all the time. Given the need to simplify an inherently complicated subject, this book is not comprehensive or definitive. Readers must not rely on this book except as a general, schematic overview. Accordingly neither the author, the editor, the publisher, the distributor, their agents, consultants nor employees accept any liability for any loss (direct or indirect, immediate or consequential, contractual or tortious) however caused from use of this book or reliance upon it.

The text in this material and any others made available by Christopher Stoakes, Viola Joseph and Christopher Stoakes Ltd does not amount to advice on a particular matter and should not be taken as such. No reliance should be placed on the content as the basis for any investment or other decision or in connection with any advice given to third parties. Please consult your appropriate professional adviser as necessary. Christopher Stoakes, Viola Joseph and Christopher Stoakes Ltd expressly disclaim all liability to any person in respect of any losses or other claims, whether direct, indirect, incidental, consequential or otherwise arising in relation to the use of these materials.

What this book is about

You want to work for a large employer – a global law, accountancy or consulting firm. Or an investment bank, or a multinational. You'll need to show you have 'commercial awareness'. But how can you if this is the first job in your career?

This book solves the conundrum. This book explains what commercial awareness is and how to demonstrate it. It also looks at how professional service firms make a profit. It shows how they win work, run projects and keep clients happy.

And if you've already got the job, this book gives you the commercial insights that will help your career.

Who this book is for

This book is for anyone interested in business. But it is particularly useful for young professionals entering the workplace for the first time. Employers expect new recruits to be commercially aware. This book tells you how.

This book is for anyone who needs to demonstrate commercial awareness in their role, but specifically for young people who are embarking on a career or are studying a vocational course where commercial awareness is required or helps.

Above all it's required reading for anyone attending an interview who may need to demonstrate an understanding of what commercial awareness is.

Who this book is by

Chris Stoakes writes best-selling books that students recommend. His books make complex subjects easy to understand and are enjoyable to read. They include *All You Need To Know About The City*, *Is Law For You?* and *Get To The Point: How To Write Well At Work*. Chris was originally a lawyer but he has since set up and run businesses on his own and with others. He has been a management consultant, marketing director and financial journalist and has taught on an MBA. Chris was a scholar at Charterhouse and Worcester College, Oxford where he read law.

CONTENTS

INTRODUCTION	7
THE BUILDING BLOCKS OF BUSINESS	
CHAPTER 1: WHAT BUSINESS IS REALLY ABOUT	9
CHAPTER 2: STRATEGY: A SENSE OF DIRECTION	17
MONEY AND ACCOUNTS	
CHAPTER 3: MONEY (1): DEBT AND EQUITY	27
CHAPTER 4: MONEY (2): ACCOUNTS	37
BEYOND BUSINESS BASICS	
CHAPTER 5: THE BUSINESS OF GOVERNMENT	51
CHAPTER 6: HOW ORGANISATIONS ARE ORGANISED	59
PROFESSIONAL SERVICE FIRMS	
CHAPTER 7: HOW PROFESSIONAL SERVICE FIRMS WORK	69
CHAPTER 8: THE 3 Ps OF PSFs	77
YOUR ROLE IN BUSINESS	
CHAPTER 9: HOW TO GET YOUR FIRST JOB	99
CHAPTER 10: MEET YOUR FIRST CLIENT	107
DEVELOPING YOUR CAREER	
CHAPTER 11: BUILDING YOUR BRAND	117
CHAPTER 12: WHAT IS COMMERCIAL AWARENESS?	129
FURTHER READING	132
INDEX / GLOSSARY	133

INTRODUCTION

This is what employers say to me about young people:

> 'They are completely useless – they come into an office environment and have no idea how to behave, how even to answer the phone properly.'

> 'The next time a job applicant tells me that they want to help deliver the organisation's strategy, I'm going to scream.'

> 'They tell me they want to get into management – but think it's just ordering people around.'

> 'When I ask a young person to do something they say they haven't been trained. But, as the person running this business, every day I face issues for which I haven't been trained.'

> 'They sound very fluent and persuasive. But if you dig deeper you find it's all a front.'

> 'They seem to think networking is about getting my email address so they can ask me for a job.'

All of which seems to me true – but also grossly unfair.

I believe your generation (by which I mean anyone under 30) is the most communication- and technology-savvy generation of all time.

You are really good at what you know and do well. But fairly rubbish at what employers seem to want.

So what to do? Read this book.

What This Book Does

This book should at the very least help you get a job – a better one than the one you might otherwise have got, and it will help you do your job better than you otherwise would. It will help you understand business and – I hope – get you interested in it. It may even change your life and fire in you a passion for business that means you start one or run one.

Business gets a bad press. It's seen as Big Brotherish, money obsessed and responsible for polluting the planet. No one with any sort of ideological or radical agenda would allow themselves to be seen sticking up for business.

Yet the majority of people in work are employees of businesses and businesses are responsible for some of the best and greatest innovations in the way we live. They attract some of the most interesting, intelligent and creative people to work in them.

And I mean business in the widest sense to include government and non-profit organisations – they all have to be 'business-like' these days.

So that's the 'commercial' bit of commercial awareness.

But I think 'awareness' means more than just being aware of business. To me it means understanding your client or customer: being 'aware' of their needs.

We all have clients these days – your first boss when you start out, then internal and external clients as your career grows (internal clients are colleagues within the organisation; external clients are 'real' clients whom the organisation serves). Your first client in your first job will be your supervisor. It will be your task to help them in their work, to anticipate what they may need of you, and to provide it to the best of your ability to make their job easier. And it's the same when you are dealing with external clients too.

This book will help you understand the business you work in (your employer), and enable you to relate to the businesses your external clients work in and represent. Whoever your clients are, this book will help you impress them through understanding what business is, what they are trying to achieve and how you can help them achieve it.

So, for me, commercial awareness is about serving your client, the person, in the context of the organisation in which they work. So there are two levels: the organisational (the business) and the personal (your client).

That's because business is not about faceless corporations. It's about people – the people you work with in your organisation and the clients you work for from other businesses. That's what makes business interesting. It's actually about people.

So that's what all of this book is about.

Who This Book Is For

This book is for people who want to work for corporates or for professional service firms. **Corporates** are big companies, for instance in manufacturing, which are also known as multinationals when they operate around the world. They buy in specialist expertise in areas such as accountancy, actuarial services, advertising, law, management consultancy, lobbying, marketing, public relations, surveying and technology, amongst others. The businesses that provide these specialist services are known as **professional service firms**.

Each needs to understand the other. The people who work in professional service firms need to understand how corporates work since these are their clients. Those who work in corporates need to know how professional service firms operate since they use them. Both need to understand business – the world in which they work. This book provides you with all you need to know.

CHAPTER 1

WHAT BUSINESS IS REALLY ABOUT

Innovation, competition and change – entrepreneurs – consumers – B2C – retail – B2B – customers – fast-moving consumer goods (FMCGs) – consumer durables – differentiate – unique selling proposition (USP) – business development (BD) – sales force – sales promotion – marketing – brand – brand management – brand extension – advertising – digital agencies – media buying – mass marketing – product placement – return on investment – marcoms – corporate identity – PR (press or public relations) – consumer research – media businesses – customer segmentation – customer value management – data mining – micromarketing – data warehouses – sales force automation – inventory management – supply chain management – logistics – time to market – product lifecycle – mass customisation – long tail effect – network effect

It's obvious isn't it?

Business is about money.

It's about making as much money as you can. No one can argue with that, can they?

Well, actually, they can. Or, at least, I can.

I don't think business is really just about money. Sure, money is important. Without it a business can't survive or thrive. Money is the oil that keeps the engine from seizing up. But it's not the fuel that gets the business from one place to another and enables it to accelerate. That's something different.

Successful businesses all have one thing in common. They produce or provide something that people want. If people don't want what you offer then you have no business. You have nothing to sell that people are willing to pay money to buy.

But if you have something that people want, pretty soon there will be other businesses offering the same sort of thing. In other words, competition. So if you want to continue to be successful you'd better improve what you're providing or offer something new that people will want.

Innovation, Competition And Change

So, you see, I think business is actually about customers, competition and innovation, and this is why it's exciting. Customers are the be-all and end-all. Without customers you have no business. But if you provide them with something they want, soon you will attract competition – others trying to have a share of your success. And the way you keep ahead of them is through innovation – giving customers even more of what they want, but better. And this is what business is really about. Because if you do it well, you will make money. And if you do it really well – better than anyone else – you will make a lot of money.

Money is a natural consequence of business success. But the best business people don't go into business to make a lot of money. They go into business because they have an idea, a vision. It's that compelling mission that makes them successful. It's why a lot of successful **entrepreneurs** (creators of successful new businesses) never stop, even when they have more money than they know what to do with. It was never about the money.

We live better these days than man has ever lived before. There is still a lot to do to enable everyone on the planet to benefit in the same way. But our food and clothing are better, our living conditions are better, and our lives are longer and less blighted by illness and pain. Life continues to get better. And that is largely down to business, making the things we want or need.

For me, the light bulb went on when I realised that almost everything I have or use in life is made or provided by business. Without business I would not have these things.

Of course, we may not even know we need them. Henry Ford, inventor of the first mass-produced motor car, said that if he had asked people what they wanted they would have said a faster horse. That isn't what he gave them. He gave them a mechanical horse, a car.

But history shows we could have had a form of car centuries before. Archimedes, the ancient Greek of Eureka fame, knew how to make a steam engine. He could have created a steam car. But back then there was no need. There was no demand for a car. What had changed by Ford's time was cities.

Lots of people lived in big cities and they were fed up with streets clogged up with horse manure. Ford gave them mechanical horses – cars – that didn't leave manure in the streets.

So to me business is about innovation – making new things we want or need, providing new services we haven't had before.

It's this emphasis on innovation and change that explains why entrepreneurs keep on going even when they've made plenty of money to retire. They crave the excitement that comes from a successful, innovative business that thrives on change.

The Quest For Customers

The best business idea will die a death if people don't want to buy it. Buyers of products or services are called customers or consumers.

Consumers are people like you and me who buy things in shops or online. Businesses that serve consumers directly are called **B2C** (business to consumer). The B2C sector is also called **retail**.

But a lot of businesses – in fact the majority – provide services to, or make things for, other businesses (which these other businesses may then sell to consumers). This is called **B2B** (business to business) and the buyers here (which are businesses) are called **customers** rather than consumers. But this isn't a hard-and-fast distinction. Consumers (people like you and me) are also called **retail customers**. When businesses sell to us it's called **retail sales**.

One way of beginning to develop your commercial awareness is by looking round you when you shop (that is, as a consumer).

When I do my weekly food shop I enjoy walking round the local supermarket. Supermarkets are amongst the most sophisticated businesses when it comes to selling to consumers. Many of the famous anecdotes in business are from supermarkets.

How in the US Wal-Mart analysed its sales and discovered that putting six packs of beer next to diapers (nappies in the UK) increased sales of both. Why? Because mums would send the dads out to buy diapers, and the dads would reward themselves by buying beer. Put diapers and beer together and you increase sales of both.

How in the UK Tesco introduced its club card (a loyalty card) which gave it access to unique insights into what its customers buy (so much so that whole books were written on the subject).

So don't think for a moment that anything about your local supermarket is there by accident.

Why are fresh fruit and vegetables at the entrance? Because it makes us feel healthy and disguises the fact that most of what a supermarket sells is processed.

Why is there that nice smell of baking by the bread section? Because they put the smell in the air-conditioning.

Why do they change the layout every few weeks? To make you look at stuff you usually walk past – but not too much otherwise we'd get irate if we couldn't find our usual stuff in roughly the usual place.

Why do they install cameras all over the place? Oh yes, for our 'health, safety and comfort'. Er, no. To see what we're looking at and to follow our random walks up and down the aisles to see where we go and why.

Is it any surprise that supermarkets moved into financial services and launched banks? They knew more about our spending habits and saw us more often than our bank did (no wonder banks started closing branches). And so on.

Take Walt Disney theme parks. They are magical places where the real world isn't allowed to intrude. So how do they keep all of those eating outlets permanently stocked up, no matter how great the demand from peak crowds? Because they truck the supplies in 24/7 through tunnels that are underground. So you never see a delivery lorry and the magical myth is maintained.

Once you start opening your eyes to what's going on around you, you start to see how clever some organisations are.

That's because they are all after your business. Next time you're in a supermarket, study the way the staff at the checkout treat you and what they say. Is that natural or have they been trained to say that? Why?

If you start looking at things this way you will soon become interested in business and this is at the heart of commercial awareness.

The stuff that a supermarket sells is called **fast-moving consumer goods** or **FMCGs**. They represent the pinnacle of marketing and sales. That thing in your hand that you picked up at the checkout may only be a chocolate bar. But behind the scenes an awful lot of people are involved in promoting it so that you buy it, especially in FMCG. There are also **consumer durables** – also known as white goods – such as fridges, freezers, washing machines, dishwashers and so on.

The makers of FMCGs and consumer durables need us to want to buy their products. It isn't enough to manufacture these things and hope consumers will buy them. Unless people have heard of them and know what makes them different they won't want to buy them. So a large part of business is about communicating the benefits of your products to consumers.

All businesses strive to **differentiate** their product or service from everybody else's so that consumers buy theirs and not those provided by competitors. The high point of differentiation is the **unique selling proposition** (**USP**) which makes you and your product stand out from the crowd. It may be better or cheaper or delivered in a different way or in a way that's more convenient. Whatever the point of differentiation is, that's your USP. It's the offer or promise you make to customers. As the CEO of a DIY tool manufacturer once said: 'In our factories we make drills. In the shops we sell holes.'

How you get your USP across to consumers is a function of **business development**.

Business Development, Marketing And Sales

Within business development (BD), a distinction is usually drawn between marketing and selling.

Selling is about getting an individual customer to buy something. This is why companies have a **sales force** – people who go round making sales on the company's behalf to customers. **Sales promotion** is about getting customers to buy things at the point-of-sale, for instance at supermarket checkouts and at petrol stations. Selling is the sharp end of marketing.

Marketing is the entire process of drawing in potential customers. It starts with getting them aware of your **brand** ('name awareness') and includes advertising, publicity, branding, customer research and segmentation. A brand is a product or service that customers will buy because it represents a promise to them or they feel something towards it; there is a relationship there.

The biggest are FMCG consumer brands that are known globally. They include Coke, McDonald's, Nike and Starbucks. Brands built up over decades represent a huge investment of money and time. They are extremely valuable.

Brands are built on points of differentiation, such as luxury, service, environmental awareness, natural ingredients and trust.

Brand management is about how you communicate and project your goods and services to the market. **Brand extension** is the name for taking an existing brand (say, a chocolate bar) and adding varieties (a new mint flavour) that refresh it.

A brand will be supported in a number of ways, for instance through **advertising**. Advertising is an industry in its own right and is led by specialist advertising agencies. These are consultancies which develop advertising campaigns for big companies and place them via national television, billboards in cities, newspapers, local radio and the internet in a planned and coordinated way to gain maximum impact for the spend. **Digital agencies** are advertising agencies that specialise in brand management online and through social media.

Advertising agencies contain people who are expert at graphic design, copywriting (making up snappy slogans which is called advertising copy) and **media buying** (placing adverts in all of these different **channels to market**). This is why advertising campaigns can cost tens of millions of pounds. They are about marketing to the mass of people out there (hence the term **mass marketing**). One form of advertising that blurs its boundaries is **product placement** where brands are placed surreptitiously in TV programmes and movies to provide subliminal promotion. A key measure will be the **return on investment** – what the company has gained in sales compared with the amount it has spent on the advertising.

BD also includes **marcoms** (marketing communications such as press releases and brochures) and **corporate identity** (the company's house style, branding and use of logos).

PR (press or public relations) at its most basic is about being quoted in the press. PR agencies specialise in placing stories that show a business or product in its best light in the media. Some also provide **consumer research**. They are commissioned by companies to find out what people really want to buy and what they think of particular products or services.

The biggest BD agencies and consultancies which do all of these things are called **media businesses**.

Customer Segmentation And Value Management

We've seen how some businesses, like supermarkets, collect a lot of data on what individual shoppers buy (for instance, through loyalty cards) and use this information to target promotions and special offers. They analyse profiles of particular types of customer and their preferences. This is called **customer segmentation** which is a way of breaking down your customer base to detect buying patterns – in order to target BD more effectively by offering customers in each segment products they are more likely to buy.

Businesses like supermarkets now look at individuals in terms of their lifetime value to the business rather than just in terms of individual transactions. This approach is called **customer value management** (turning each interaction with a customer into an opportunity to learn more about, and sell more to, that customer). Every time you go into the supermarket you may spend only £20. But if you go there three times a week, that's £3,000 a year and over ten years that's £30,000. That's big business from just one customer.

These efforts to focus more specifically on individuals' wants and needs generate huge amounts of data which need to be interrogated by algorithms to detect patterns. This is called **data mining**. Banks, for instance, use it to detect risk and default trends by customer type amongst portfolios of hundreds of thousands of loans made to different customers. Retailers use it to segment customers by buying habits and patterns (known as **micromarketing**). Repositories of these vast amounts of data are called **data warehouses**.

Sales force automation enables information about products and orders to be kept up-to-date minute-by-minute and made available at all contact points simultaneously (sales force, call centre, local branch, head office, after-sales service, complaints). This gives a company a so-called 360-degree view of each customer and means that whenever you call and whoever you speak to at a company, they can have instant access to your up-to-date customer profile.

Inventory And Supply Chain Management

Having lured your customer in, you need to make sure you have the products they want available. Making sure you have the right stock in the right amounts is a specialist skill called **inventory management** (stock is called **inventory**). It's part of **supply chain management** (also known as **logistics**) which is about getting stock from the factories (wherever they are in the world) to the retail outlet (or the customer's door) as quickly and efficiently as possible.

Supply chain management brings together the processes linking marketing and sales with production, the physical facilities involved (factories, warehouses, trucks, ships and airfreight) and the technology that helps to plan, manage and predict customer demand. All these things involve trade-offs – between manufacturing flexibility and location, distribution cost and inventory holding.

For example, Wal-Mart (previously mentioned) was one of the first businesses to automate everything from its checkout tills to its storage sites. This meant it knew exactly how much of every item it had and where. So, when there was a snow storm on the east coast of the States, it could move all of its stock of winter items (gloves, snow shovels and so on) from all of its other outlets across the country to its east coast stores overnight, ready for when its shops opened the next day. This may not sound like much but in reality it is a massive and – at the time –

extraordinary undertaking. A more everyday example: when you pass a lorry on the motorway, think about what it's carrying and to where. Sophisticated logistics will ensure that it doesn't return empty.

Estimating how many products to make to meet expected demand, taking into account seasonal fluctuations and the transportation time, can lead to massive over- or under-production which in turn can make a business go bust. It's mission-critical stuff.

The impact of online sales and the explosion in customer data mean that businesses need to know exactly what customers want and deliver it almost instantly.

The speed at which products are designed, manufactured and distributed has accelerated. For instance, fashion retailers compete to get new designs out in a matter of days. This is called **time to market** and tracks the time taken to get a product from the drawing board into customers' hands.

This in turn means that products have a much more limited life as the pace of change and innovation increases. **Product lifecycle** is about how long it takes for a product to go out of date or out of fashion and become obsolete.

Mass customisation is the idea that a commoditised, mass-market product can be tailored to the customer's specific wants, so creating a personalised product.

This means that profit isn't necessarily generated – as it once was – through selling the same thing to millions of people. On the contrary, the **long tail effect** is the idea that items with a very select market can still make money – which was how Amazon started (originally it sold books and claimed to have 'infinite shelf space').

However, some products depend on the **network effect** to become market dominant. So, for example, the first person to have a telephone had no one to call. As more people owned them, the benefit multiplied. So with social media.

Right, so you've got your product, you've identified your target market and you're reaching it. Sales are increasing. Things are looking great. What else do you need?

For many businesses the answer is: not much. But don't forget: if your product is popular and you attract a lot of customers, there will be competitors out there who want a slice of your pie. To fight back you need a plan. In business a plan is called a strategy (although this is now a much-abused term; people seem to have strategies for getting out of bed). Strategy is what we look at next.

CHAPTER 2

STRATEGY: A SENSE OF DIRECTION

Strategy – Peter Drucker – theory of the business – vision – mission – culture – models – process – SWOT analysis – strengths, weaknesses, opportunities and threats – Porter's Five Forces – competitors – buyers – suppliers – new entrants – substitutes – Boston Consulting Group – BCG Product or Growth-Share Matrix – external environment – PESTL – convergence of platforms and content – software as a service (SaaS) – channels to market – bricks 'n' clicks – disintermediation – barriers to entry – disruptive technology – secular trends – step changes – paradigm shifts – consumerism – globalisation – multinational companies (MNCs) – the knowledge economy – professional service firms – knowledge workers – knowledge management – intellectual property rights (IPR) – core – non-core – outsourcing – offshoring – near-shoring – business process re-engineering (BPR) – enterprise resource planning (ERP) – best practice – best-in-class – just-in-time production – continuous improvement or kaizen – scenario planning

More business books are devoted to the subject of strategy and how to do it than anything else. But at heart strategy is simple. It's nothing more or less than a plan. It tells you what you should be doing and – as importantly – what not.

When I became a marketing director I had an impossible job. All sorts of senior people in the organisation came to me to ask for funds from my marketing budget to help promote the business in one way or another. I had no way of judging whether what they were proposing was going to take the business in the right direction. And that's because we had no explicit strategy.

After a while the people at the top – at my suggestion and that of others – launched a strategic review. It took a year and was in-depth. At the end we had a strategy: a direction in which all involved wanted to take the business. That strategy pointed to three or four key priorities: things we had to focus on in order to get to where we wanted to go. Overnight my job became easier and meaningful. Now when people came to me with appeals to spend money I could match what they were proposing against our list of priorities. If it wasn't one of the priorities it didn't get the cash.

In any business it's not a lack of ideas that holds the business back. Usually there are plenty of ideas about what the business could and should be doing and the direction in which it should go. No, the real enemy is trying to do too many things all at once: a scatter-shot approach which means that nothing in particular is focused on for any length of time, which means that nothing is ever properly achieved.

So for me **strategy** is a plan and a list of priorities. A business cannot expand in every direction at once. It doesn't have the money, the people, the time or the expertise. Developing a list of priorities can be painful. Some people will be disappointed. They may even leave, realising that they are better off in a business where what they want to do is considered more important. But that will simply help this business to streamline itself and focus on what it does best.

The Theory Of The Business

Strategy doesn't have to be explicit. There doesn't even need to be a written-down plan. Peter Drucker, possibly the most famous and influential management thinker there's ever been, said that all businesses make implicit assumptions about their USP and their customers whether they articulate it in a strategy (plan) or not. He called this the **theory of the business** without which you don't have a business at all.

So it's perfectly possible to be in business and not have a strategy or to have one that is only implicit. But businesses that have an explicit strategy tend to have a greater sense of energy and purpose. Everybody in the business knows what the goals are and everyone pulls together as a team to achieve them.

The people in the business have a sense of direction, of momentum. They know what makes them different (what the USP is) and this helps them set a course or direction which will enable them to succeed. By having a plan they know how to communicate what they are to the outside world – their market – and everyone in the organisation is able to work towards the same end.

The business knows what it is trying to achieve and how best to achieve it, which means resources get applied in the most efficient way to its commercial objectives.

Putting A Man On The Moon

The language of strategy includes the terms **vision** and **mission** and these can be confusing. To my mind, the strategic vision is a picture of what the business will look like in a number of years' time or what it will have achieved. Words may be used to convey this vision but in essence it's pictorial. You can see it. It's immediate.

There is a story, no doubt apocryphal, that a US president was doing a tour of the US space programme (called NASA). This was in the 1960s before the lunar landings. Seeing a man who was sweeping the floors, the President asked him what he was doing (sounds unlikely, I know: it's obvious what he was doing – sweeping the floors). But the floor sweeper is supposed to have replied (and this is the point of the story): 'I'm helping to get a man on the moon.'

That was NASA's vision: putting a man on the moon; and everyone from top to bottom in the organisation knew it.

If vision is where we are going to, mission is how we get there. It's a statement of how we will do what we do to achieve our vision. It's often to do with an organisation's **culture**, defined by management consultants McKinsey as the 'way we do things around here'. So it's a bit evangelical. It's about how the organisation differentiates itself in achieving that vision – how the organisation will do things differently from the rest of the market to achieve that vision.

General Electric's mission after World War Two was to put a fridge in every house in America (at a time when few had them). Bill Gates's mission when he founded Microsoft was to put a computer in every home (this was at a time when people thought the world would be run by half-a-dozen massive mainframes and computers were very much confined to the workplace). Steve Jobs wanted to put a thousand songs in your pocket (the iPod).

For its mission to be successful, GE had to find ways of manufacturing and marketing fridges on a mass-produced basis. Gates had to develop a universal operating system. Jobs had to develop a design that was so elegant and intuitive a child could use it without a manual.

The mission is the way the vision is achieved and it's also what makes the organisation stand out. It's what makes it innovative. The mission is about passion. It encapsulates the desire to change, which is why it is evangelical.

Strategy And Commercial Awareness

In terms of commercial awareness, strategy is always a good topic to talk to a prospective employer about, both to ascertain whether it has a strategy and to demonstrate that you know what strategy is. You don't want to commit your career to a business that is directionless.

But don't overstep the mark. Don't talk about 'helping to deliver' the business's strategy. You can't. And while you remain fairly junior in an organisation whatever you do will only have an indirect impact on the business overall. Your personal strategy should be to do your job as best you can and let others worry about how it fits with the business's overall aims.

So what are the elements of business strategy?

Models And Process

This is where I want to introduce you to the idea of business **models** and to the idea of **process**. Both are crucial terms in business.

A model is a way of looking at an issue and is usually based on years of academic research. The model will break an issue down into its component parts. Models are also often pictorial. In a sense models provide the 'what'.

Process provides the 'how'. Process is the way in which you get something done.

Often a failure of strategy is a failure of process. The organisation didn't know how to go about developing a strategy or how to get it accepted by everyone or how to make it happen (execute it) once it had been drawn up.

Models and process work hand in hand. A model helps you identify what it is you are trying to do, the bits you need to consider. Process helps you focus on how to do it.

Let's look at some well-known strategic models.

SWOT

The simplest and most well-known is the **SWOT analysis**. SWOT stands for **strengths, weaknesses, opportunities** and **threats**.

SWOT helps an organisation to look internally (within) at what it does well (its strengths) and where it needs to improve (its weaknesses) and to look externally (outside) at the opportunities (for instance, to gain new customers or enter new markets) and the threats (for instance, competitors or changes in the external environment).

SWOT has come in for a fair amount of criticism over the years. Critics say it is simplistic and subjective.

But in my experience as a management consultant, one of the big issues around strategy is one of process: how do you get an organisation or the people in an organisation to start to look at the organisation in strategic terms. SWOT is a good place to start. It poses simple but big questions. What are we good at? Where do we fall down? What are the opportunities open to us out in the market? What are the big external threats to our business?

And – also a process issue – you can use it to involve everyone in an organisation (again in my experience the more junior the staff the more aware they are of the organisation's issues). And it scales well. You can use it at a small, departmental level and right across the whole organisation. So a supermarket can apply SWOT to an individual store and to its entire business.

Porter's Five Forces

Michael Porter, a management academic, studied many businesses and realised that common forces influence their success. His model, **Porter's Five Forces**, identifies them as:

- Your industry **competitors**,
- Who your **buyers** (customers) are (they will try to force down the price at which they buy from you) and
- Your **suppliers** (they will try to force up the price at which they sell the raw commodities you need to produce finished goods).

So far so obvious. But then he hit upon two other forces that businesses need to be mindful of. These are:

- **New entrants** – new competitors who will enter your market because they spot rich pickings (at your expense) and
- **Substitutes** – people who will decide they can do without your product because they can do it themselves or find alternatives.

If you're seeking a job at a company, you should think about its business in these terms. Its top people certainly will. Supermarkets moving into financial services are new entrants. People who sell their house by listing it online rather than using a traditional estate agent are substitutes.

BCG Product Matrix

Another famous business model was created by **Boston Consulting Group** (a management consultancy) and it's called the **BCG Product or Growth-Share**

Matrix. Most businesses have more than one product or service line and the BCG model helps them work out which to invest in. The two key factors are: how much market share do you have (as against your competitors); and is this market fast-growing or mature?

- Mature markets necessarily do not offer much further growth. So if you have a *small share* of a *mature market*, there's no point in focusing much effort there. In fact BCG calls it a 'dog' and says you should get rid of it ('divest').
- But if you have a *big share* of a *mature market*, BCG calls this a 'cash cow' (because it makes good money and provides a steady income flow) and says you should use this to generate funds to invest in fast-growing markets.
- If you have a *big share* of a *fast-growing market* you need to focus your efforts (and investment) here. These are what BCG calls 'stars'.
- Finally there are *fast-growing markets* in which you have a *small share* (maybe because you've held back because you're not sure whether they are going to turn into big markets worth the effort). BCG calls these 'question marks' – you need to decide whether to invest fully to grow your share and become a star or get out before you risk becoming a dog.

External Environment

What all useful strategy models do is get businesses to look outside themselves. A business cannot devise a strategy in a vacuum. It has to think about the world around it and how this is changing.

So, for example, the biggest forces changing our world can be grouped under the headings: political, economic, social, technological and legal (known amongst management experts as **PESTL**). At any one time one or more of these will be uppermost in shaping your markets. For example, when China opened up internationally, the greatest factor was political. As a new middle class emerged in India it was social. For the world as a whole, over the past thirty years it has been technological.

Examples Of Technological Change

It's hard to remember that in the past people used to look at a small box in the corner of their sitting room to get all the information and entertainment they needed from the outside world.

The television has been replaced by a **convergence of platforms** as television, computers, video games, internet access and mobile phones all started to be provided through the same device, and television programmes, broadcast at a particular time (and without, in those days, the ability to record them), have been replaced by a **convergence of content**, as films, music, television, video games and news all started to be streamed. Similarly, applications no longer reside on computers but together with content are stored in the computing cloud and are instantly accessible whenever and wherever you want (**software as a service** or **SaaS**).

The internet offered businesses new **channels to market** (ways of reaching their customers) so that it became common for retailers to have both actual, physical shops as well as online portals (a strategy known as **bricks 'n' clicks**).

The web also allowed **disintermediation** – the by-passing – of conventional businesses. Traditional 'publishers' ranging from newspapers to radio stations and record companies were disintermediated in this way. Newspapers became online streams with news delivered in real time and creating whole new industries of blogging, vlogging and podcasting.

People were no longer passive consumers of information. They became active in its creation. Wikis (web pages that allowed anyone to log into them and change them) enabled collaboration and the sharing of knowledge on a mass scale with few attendant costs.

The key is how to monetise these innovations (turn them into money) which has led to new business models (new ways of doing business) such as subscription services and streamed services that survive on advertising revenue.

Business leaders have to be aware all the time of how these factors will affect their business and whether these will lower **barriers to entry** allowing more competitors in. If technology has a fundamental and immediate impact it is called **disruptive technology** – it changes the competitive landscape and channels to market overnight.

Secular Trends And Paradigm Shifts

There are other big trends (often called **secular trends**) shaping our future (where these lead to significant change they are called **step changes** or **paradigm shifts**).

For example, we've talked about supermarkets which are symbolic of the rise of **consumerism**, the idea that everyone is a buyer whose needs are there to be addressed. Shopping used to be a way of buying the boring things needed to live.

But with the explosion in fashion, food and entertainment, shopping malls became leisure destinations where people went for a day out. When people switched to shopping online, shopping malls needed to work harder at selling an experience, a place to socialise in real time and space with friends.

Another big business trend is **globalisation**; the idea that the world is becoming a smaller place and we will all end up buying the same products and services. Major companies do a lot of business outside their home country, in search of new markets and more consumers. The biggest businesses of all, which trade all over the world, are called **multinational companies** or **MNCs**.

The Knowledge Economy

Perhaps the biggest paradigm shift in business has been the move towards service economies and away from manufacturing. Service businesses are know-how businesses. Their USP is what they know – their expertise in providing the service, their knowledge of who their customers are, and how to address their specific needs.

It's clear that **professional service firms** are know-how businesses: accountants, lawyers, consultants, and so on, sell their expertise. But the idea of the knowledge economy (a term invented by Peter Drucker) goes wider than this.

An oil company may think that its assets such as oil rigs, refineries and pipelines are what keep it in business. But as Drucker would have pointed out, it's knowing where to drill for oil that matters. A farmer may think that it's his land and work that are key to being successful. But, again, Drucker would have said it's the farmer's knowledge of when and where to plant crops and how to rotate them that is crucial.

The pillars of capitalism used to be money (capital), the means of production (equipment) and an abundance of cheap labour (employees). But nowadays people recognise that technology has reduced the cost of production and that competitive advantage depends not on how much you make and at what price, but on what you know.

Your employees are no longer just muscle and brawn needed to operate machines; they are now **knowledge workers**. Companies recognise that what their employees carry round in their heads is critical to the business.

If what matters is what you know, it follows that businesses need to try to record and store this information and make it available organisation-wide. This is called **knowledge management**.

Businesses now have chief information officers (CIOs) and know-how managers whose role is to capture and organise the business's knowledge and to focus on how to record, store and share it.

This is related to the increasing importance of **intellectual property rights** (**IPR**) – these are the legally-protected inventions and innovations which in a knowledge economy can be a business's principal source of differentiation. They include patents, trade marks, copyrights and licences. They can be technological (an app), visual (Nike's swoosh) or artistic (such as books and songs).

A company's IPR can be its single most important asset. It's the licence fees for using Windows that have made Bill Gates as rich as he is. It's Nike's swoosh that is its USP.

Being Attuned To The External Environment

Strategy models help organisations stay attuned to their external environment and how it is changing. There is a strategy model by Robert Grant that says simply that strategy is an iterative process between an organisation and its external environment. In other words, as the external environment changes, the successful business changes and adapts to it, even anticipates it.

This is crucial to a business's survival, especially as the pace of change itself accelerates. It's tempting to think that the biggest companies in the world don't change. But in fact the corporate landscape is changing all the time as companies get taken over, shrink and go bust. The top 100 UK companies by size (the formal term is 'market capitalisation') constitute what's called the FTSE 100 (short for *Financial Times* Stock Exchange 100 – the SE compiles it and the *FT* publishes it). But if you look back 10 years, only just over half the companies in the FTSE 100 ten years ago are still there now. In other words, almost half have disappeared. This is how relentless the impact of competition and the pace of change are.

All businesses regularly re-evaluate what is **core** (crucial) and what is **non-core** to their business. They may decide that non-core parts of their business can be subcontracted to an external supplier – a business that specialises in, say, providing HR support to other businesses. This is called **outsourcing**. Relocating (some of) your functions to another, cheaper country is called **offshoring** or **near-shoring**.

Business Process Re-engineering

Rethinking how things are done in your business is called **business process re-engineering** (**BPR**) and may be accompanied by importing integrated technology packages (called **enterprise resource planning** or **ERP**) that join up all of your underlying processes and functions. All businesses have common basic administrative functions (such as HR, Technology and Finance). The idea behind ERP is that you can buy a software suite that will do all of this for you in a way that reflects **best practice** across industry (often called **best-in-class**).

This quest for business efficiency (improving profitability by reducing costs) has led to waves of production innovation in the last half-century including **just-in-time production** and **continuous improvement** (also known as **kaizen**), both of which were developed in Japan.

With just-in-time production you don't hold big inventories of stock – instead you have only what you need immediately to hand.

Scenario Planning

The best business leaders are thinking about their businesses and how they can improve them all the time. One of the best strategy models for this is **scenario planning**, created by Arie de Geus. At the time that he devised it, companies had big planning departments. At one point Sony said it had a 500-year business plan. But de Geus said this approach was wrong. It was wrong because no one can predict the future. What matters is not how accurate your prediction is, but what you are able to do about it when the future happens. This is the basis of scenario planning, which is also called 'what if' planning.

Instead of trying to predict the future, you imagine a series of possible scenarios that might unfold and plan how you would address each one if it were to happen – as in: 'What would we need to do if.....?' This set of plans then becomes part of your strategy: when one of these eventualities comes to pass, you reach into your desk drawer for the appropriate plan of action that you have already thought about in advance.

Whether these scenarios actually happen is almost irrelevant. The point is that they make an organisation light on its feet. It gets into the habit of thinking about where the threats and opportunities lie.

Businesses which are successful in coping with the future are able to do so not because they can predict it but because they have learnt how to cope with its uncertainties. This is why large companies have ditched their formal planning departments in favour of something more dynamic, able to deal with previously unforeseen business disruptions.

So, we've got our strategy sorted. We've got our vision and mission. We know our priorities. We know the things we'd like to do but for which we don't have time and resource just yet. We'll put them on the back burner. For now our strategy tells us the three or four things we need to focus on to be successful (any more than three or four and they are no longer priorities).

Good. Now what we need to do is focus on what shape our business is and, yes, finally, how money works within it. That's what we do next.

CHAPTER 3

MONEY (1): DEBT AND EQUITY

Start-up capital – working capital – profit – sole trader – partnership – personal liability – incorporated – insolvent – private company – SMEs (small and medium size enterprises) – public companies – equities – equity – principal – interest – servicing the debt – commercial bank – retail banking – secured lending – leverage – gearing – dividends – economies of scale – unit cost – cash flow – venture capitalists (VCs) – three Fs – franchising – private equity – unicorns – name recognition – going public, listing, floating, initial public offering (IPO) – takeover or M&A – bidder – target – wholly-owned subsidiary – diversification – consolidation – competition law – dominant market positions – monopolies – investment bank – management buy outs (MBOs)

If money isn't the point of business, where does money fit in? In three ways.

You need money to be in business. This is called **start-up capital**.

You need money to stay in business. This is called **working capital**.

And, if you're to thrive, you need to make a **profit**, so you can reinvest in the business, make it better and reward your investors. It's this last which makes people think that business is just about making money, by which they mean profit.

But money has a far more interesting part to play, in enabling a business to start and in allowing it to expand and grow.

But first we need to look at the shape of our business. For a start, what actually is it?

Business Formats

Businesses can take many forms. I can set up in business as Chris Stoakes Window Cleaner without any more formality than filing a tax return. This is called being a **sole trader** (an individual). A lot of businesses are one-person businesses like this.

If I go into business with one or more others this is called a **partnership** (several individuals working together). Again there is little formality involved. Under the law the very fact of working together to try to make a profit is sufficient to create a partnership. But it would be wise to have some sort of agreement between us to avoid disputes in the future.

Both of these business formats have one big downside: **personal liability**. As a sole trader I am my business. If the business fails I am responsible for all of its debts even if this makes me bankrupt. In a partnership every partner has joint and several liability: we are all liable together (joint) but each one of us is also liable on his or her own (several) for all of the partnership's debts. This can be risky.

Companies

This is why businesses are generally **incorporated** (that is, they are companies). You can tell if a business is a company because it has 'Limited' or 'Ltd' at the end of its name. This is to warn those dealing with it that its liability is limited.

This means that if the company becomes **insolvent** (goes bust) the owners and those who work in it won't be liable for its debts.

Let's say a group of ten people start a company with £100 contributed equally by them (£10 each). If the company uses up all of that £100 and then goes bust they won't be liable even though they, as shareholders, own the company. They've each lost their £10, for sure. But they won't have to pay in any more to pay off the company's debts.

Once a shareholder has put in their share of the capital they are no longer liable if the company goes bust (nor, usually, are the directors). So if a company has capital of £100 and, say, ten equal shareholders, once I have put in my £10 I am not liable for anything more.

So what, you say.

So big deal. When this came about in 1854 in the Joint Stock Companies Act it had a massive impact on business. It meant entrepreneurs could set up in business doing new and risky things and not lose all of their or their shareholders' money. It was crucial for innovation.

Some of the largest professional service firms in accountancy, law and management consultancy were originally partnerships. They have since converted into LLPs (**limited liability partnerships**). LLPs preserve the culture of a business partnership while providing limited liability for the individual partners.

Private And Public Companies

You can set up a business as a company quite cheaply. You can buy a company 'off the shelf' from a company formation agent or form it directly at Companies House, the UK company register.

This book is published by my company, Christopher Stoakes Limited (have a look at the small print at the front). You'll see the use of the word 'limited' in its name. This tells you it's a company 'incorporated with limited liability' – the liability is limited to the share capital. This warns those who do business with me that my business has limited liability and I am not personally liable.

My company is a **private company**. There are thousands and thousands of private companies doing all sorts of different things. Each is owned by a small number of shareholders who generally run the business and are directors in it. These companies are **SMEs** (**small and medium size enterprises**).

But the biggest businesses are **public companies** (they generally have the letters 'PLC' or 'plc' after their names meaning 'public limited company'). They are called 'public' because their shares can be bought by the public, and are freely traded on a stock exchange. The colloquial term for a big company these days is a **corporate**.

By contrast I can't buy shares in a private company – there is no market for such shares – and I would need to approach an existing shareholder who would be unlikely to want to sell just because I showed up.

Equity In Companies

Shares that investors hold in companies are often called **equities** and **equity** is the term for a shareholder's stake in the business. If a company is successful and grows, the worth of a shareholding – an equity stake – will grow with it. If I have a 10% stake in a company worth £100,000, my equity is worth £10,000. If the company grows and so it is worth £200,000, my shares are now worth £20,000. My equity in it has doubled in value.

Debt

Equity is not the only form of capital (money) that a company can use. The other – which you probably know more about – is debt.

Debt is a loan. The lender lends an amount of money (often called the **principal**, which is short for 'principal amount' – meaning the amount borrowed) and the borrower pays the lender **interest** on the loan. This interest rewards the lender for making the loan. The act of paying interest on the loan is called **servicing** the debt.

Lenders are usually banks. A lending bank takes in deposits and lends those deposits out again. The market name for a lending bank (especially when lending to business) is a **commercial bank**. By contrast **retail banking** is about lending to and dealing with the public. Most big lending banks do both commercial and retail banking.

Sometimes the lender will want to take a charge over the business for making the loan. This is just like a mortgage in a home loan. It means that if the borrower defaults (fails to pay) the lender can sell the business or bits of it to recover what the lender is owed. These loans are called secured loans or **secured lending**.

Businesses use debt because it helps them to expand. Let's say I have £100,000 with which I can buy a studio flat. But for £200,000 I could buy a one-bed flat which will be easier to sell and is likely to increase in value more quickly. I borrow the extra £100,000 I don't have and buy the one-bed flat for £200,000.

After a year it has gone up in value to £250,000 (an increase of 25%) while the studio has gone up in value to £110,000 (an increase of 10%). I sell the one-bed flat and repay the mortgage (which is what a home loan is called). Borrowing that £100,000 has gained me £50,000. Without it I would have made a gain of only £10,000. That is the power of leverage. Of course, I need to be able to pay the interest on that £100,000 loan.

The use of debt in business is called **leverage** or **gearing**. Debt, like the gears on a bicycle, can accelerate a business's development.

Interest And Dividends

Let's look at debt and equity from the point of view of the provider. The lender of the debt will receive interest during the loan and will have the principal amount returned at the end of the loan. They will not get back more than the amount lent and the interest on it.

Now let's look at the equity investors. They will invest in the company in return for shares. Their hope is that the company expands, increases in value and that their shareholdings become more valuable. A company that makes a profit may choose to pay some or all of that profit out to its shareholders as **dividends**. A dividend is income paid in respect of a share (a bit like interest in respect of a loan).

But companies aren't obliged to pay dividends. It depends on whether they make a profit (as opposed to a loss) and whether they want to pay that profit out to shareholders rather than re-invest it in the business (to make the business bigger or better). So whereas a lender can expect interest, a shareholder can only hope for a dividend.

Why Companies Use Debt

Debt and equity are crucial to businesses. Businesses need money to expand. And they need to expand because if they don't they will be overtaken by other companies – their competition – that do.

Generally in business (but not always), the bigger you are the cheaper you can produce your goods and services. This is called **economies of scale**. You can buy in your raw materials more cheaply and produce in greater volume so your **unit cost** goes down. This doesn't always happen. The bigger a business the more complex it can be to manage, so you can get 'diseconomies of scale'. But generally in business, bigger is better – a bigger business is better able to withstand shocks and see off competitors.

Businesses can be big users of debt – more, proportionately, than we as individuals would be. This is because, at least historically, the interest that a business pays on a loan is 'tax deductible'. This means the business deducts the interest it has paid from its profits before those profits are taxed. This is because all costs of a business are deducted from its income to determine what the profit is (and interest is a cost). By contrast, dividends to shareholders are generally paid out of taxed profit. So debt can be cheaper for companies than equity.

Cash Flow Versus Profit

You might think that a business that is doing well and is profitable can expand using its profit. Often it can. But this profit (once it's translated into cash) may not be enough. The biggest risk to a business (especially the smaller it is) is that it runs out of cash. You see, a business can be profitable but still go bust.

How come?

Let's say we decide to start an artisan corner-shop. It's basically a small metro-style store but selling only organic and craft-made food. We choose a large town or city which is affluent enough to support such a shop.

We have a lot of immediate costs to meet – fitting out the shop, buying in stock, hiring and paying staff and marketing (advertising the shop and using PR to raise its profile locally). To fund this we take out a loan and maybe raise equity by launching the business as a company: we sell a few shares to family and friends. So far so good.

Suppose the shop is a massive success and we realise we need to expand. We need to launch in other sites around town. We need to expand to other cities. We need to do this before someone else decides we're on to a good thing and launches a competitor. We might be tempted to expand on the back of what our single, existing outlet is making by way of profit. To do so could be a costly mistake. Our existing shop is unlikely to be bringing in enough cash to fund rapid expansion.

Rick Stein

This is why, bizarrely, small businesses are most at risk when they seem to be at the height of success. Rick Stein, the TV chef, almost went out of business early in his restaurant career. He had a small harbourside restaurant in Padstow. He bought whatever the local fishermen caught and his customers, also local, ate whatever he served. Then his very first cookbook (long before he was on TV) became a hit and won a foodie prize.

Suddenly the Chelsea set were coming down to Padstow to eat in his restaurant. First he had to cope with the increase in customers – he had to add tables, fit a bigger kitchen and hire more staff. Then he discovered these people expected a proper menu with a lot of choice and weren't just going to eat whatever the local fishermen had caught that day. So he had to buy in a lot more fish and throw a lot more away, uneaten. These extra demands on his existing **cash flow** almost bankrupted him. And yet to the outside world his business was booming and getting bigger.

Taking Off Is When A Business Is Most At Risk

It's a bit like a small plane taking off. The point at which it's leaving the runway and getting into the air – when everything is looking great, it's accelerating and lifting off – is also the most dangerous. A drop in air speed or a sideways gust and it can crash back to earth. So with business.

This is why, at least for small businesses, cash flow is often more important than profit – at least until a business is properly up and running. Then it can focus on making a big enough profit to reinvest and reward its shareholders with dividends.

Profit Is Not Necessary All The Time

And there's another odd thing about profit. You don't have to make a profit all the time. Some businesses make losses for year after year but still go on. Let's say I make steel. I have a lot of customers so I sell a lot of steel. But often the price I get barely covers my costs.

One year I can make a profit, the next year a loss. Let's say my turnover is £100 million. On that basis I can probably borrow £20 million. Let's say that for a number of years I make a loss of £1 million a year. With that loan of £20 million I can stay in business for 20 years. Again, it's my cash flow that is keeping me in business.

The way I look at it is like this: cash flow is the cash I have in the till at the end of the day when I close my artisan corner-shop. Have I got enough to pay tomorrow's bills? If so, I'm OK. Profit is what my accountants tell me I've made or not made every quarter. Every three months they add up my income and outgoings. Sometimes I make a profit, sometimes a loss. But if my day-to-day cash flow is fine then I'm not too worried. Profit can come once you've got cash flow sorted.

Venture Capital

You can see that start-ups can be risky, which is why there are specialist investors called **venture capitalists** (**VCs**) that provide equity funding (venture capital) to start-ups in return for a shareholding (think *Dragons' Den*).

I mentioned earlier that I initially sold shares in my start-up business to family and friends. Venture capital providers, who are professional investors, refer to these informal sources of initial equity capital as the **three Fs** (family, friends and fools) – because this sort of investment is risky. Hence 'venture' (risky) 'capital' (money).

So why do VCs do it?

The answer is that small, fast-growing companies, if successful, can provide great returns to investors. VCs are expert at evaluating whether a small business is likely to be successful. Once it reaches a certain size they will sell their shares and reinvest the proceeds in other small start-ups. So their business is investing in small businesses (and then selling at a profit in order to invest in others).

Two out of three businesses fail before they are five years old. So a VC provider will want a big stake in any investee company to compensate for the other two that go bust.

Franchising As A Business Format

A business format that addresses cash flow is **franchising**. It involves franchisors and franchisees.

A franchisor has a product or service with a particular brand that the franchisor wants to expand quickly (to gain increased market presence) without the enormous capital outlay involved.

A franchisee is someone keen to get into business but without necessarily having a new product or service they particularly want to sell.

The franchisor and franchisee enter into a franchise agreement under which the franchisor makes available to the franchisee the business format in return for a regular payment (royalty) for the franchisee's use of the business idea and get-up (how it looks and is delivered).

Franchise agreements can be complex. The franchisee may be required to buy everything needed in the business from the franchisor, which can be expensive. The franchisor is reliant on the franchisee to make a success of the business – otherwise a tatty, poorly-performing outlet may damage the brand.

You'd be surprised how many businesses are based on franchising. The most famous franchise is McDonald's. Ray Kroc, the founder, discovered that two brothers (called McDonald) were selling beef burgers from their cattle ranch. He got them to develop their brand (the golden arches) into a franchise which he then built into a global business.

The benefit for the customer is the implicit promise of the same quality of product and service at every franchised outlet. The benefit for the franchisee is the immediate benefit of an existing brand without the need for enormous initial marketing. The benefit for the franchisor is rapid expansion. The bigger the number of franchisees a business has, the greater its brand impact.

Building The Business

Let's assume that when we started our business we attracted venture capital funding. Now our VC backers have decided they want out. They want to realise their investment and reinvest the profit in other start-ups. After all, that's what they specialise in: they identify successful future businesses and back them.

What then for us?

There are two avenues we can go down. We can remain privately owned. Our VC backers might sell their stakes in our business to a **private equity** fund. A private equity fund raises money from institutional investors such as pension funds and insurance companies and invests it in fast-growing companies.

Some companies, for instance in the biotech field, spend years developing products for which they need a great deal of capital investment. They look to VC and private equity. There are tech start-ups that become **unicorns** (companies valued at $1 billion or more which remain privately owned).

Going Public

The other avenue is to become a public company. This means listing on a stock exchange. Often companies do this to exploit and expand upon their brand's impact in the market. It's about **name recognition**.

If you have an identifiable brand that is widely known amongst your customer base, then you can exploit the financial benefits of this by going public. **Going public**, **listing**, **floating**, doing an **IPO** (**initial public offering**) all mean the same thing. They mean listing your shares on a stock exchange so the public can buy them.

This will allow your VC investors to sell their shares (and you, as the founder of the business, to turn part of your shareholding and hard work into cash) and allow others – including customers – to buy into your business.

In this way your business's profile in the financial markets can match and build on your business's brand amongst customers.

Being able to tap the financial markets will allow you to raise further finance to continue expanding your business. In particular, as a public company, you can issue bonds. Bonds are a form of efficient debt funding. They tend to be – but aren't always – cheaper for borrowers than loans because bonds are designed to be sold and transferred in the financial markets. Holders of bonds can sell them on more easily than loans so bonds tend to command a lower rate of interest – also good for your expansion.

Mergers & Acquisitions (M&A)

One other advantage of going public is that your company's shares now have an instant value because they can be sold on the stock exchange at any time. This makes it much easier to buy other companies.

When one company buys another it's called a **takeover** or an **M&A** deal (M&A stands for 'mergers & acquisitions'). The acquiring company (the **bidder**) wants to buy all of the shares of the company to be acquired (called the **target**) in order to make it a **wholly-owned subsidiary**. So the bidder will offer shares in itself to the target's shareholders in return for their shares in the target. This way they will become shareholders in the bidder (which will then be an enlarged group that also has the target within it) or they can sell the shares on the stock exchange.

Companies use M&A deals as a more direct way of moving into a new area of business (called **diversification**) without having to go through the whole start-up cycle. Or they use it to buy a business in the same sector to increase their market presence. This is called **consolidation**. There is usually a whole body of regulation called **competition law** that governs whether, and the extent to which, a company can consolidate. This is because a company that has too great a market share can start to control (increase) prices, which is bad for consumers. The purpose of competition law is to prevent **dominant market positions** and **monopolies**.

Companies involved in takeovers usually appoint an **investment bank** to advise them. Investment banks don't lend money. Instead they advise companies on M&A deals and how to fund them – for instance through issuing new shares or debt in the form of bonds. The investment bank will distribute those securities (the collective name for shares and bonds) and trade them.

Following a takeover, the acquiring company may sell off bits of the target that it doesn't want. These businesses are often bought by the previous managers (who know the business well and want the chance to make the most of it) in deals that are called **MBOs (management buy outs)**. The managers won't have the money to buy the business. Instead they may seek venture capital funding and in return give shares in the business they are buying to the venture capital provider. Which completes the loop.

So far we've looked at money as capital: the debt and equity that companies need to establish, maintain and expand their businesses. Now we're going to take a closer look at the accounts that companies produce and, in particular, at how they work out whether they are making a profit.

CHAPTER 4

MONEY (2): ACCOUNTS

Income statement – profit and loss account (P&L) – balance sheet – fixed assets – current assets – retained earnings – return on capital employed (ROCE) – return on investment (ROI) – gross profit – net profit – margin – fixed costs – overheads – variable costs – depreciation – amortisation – profit – ebitda – cash flow statement – working capital requirement – factoring – invoice discounting – supply chain finance – receivables – hire purchase – conditional sale – asset finance – revolving credit facility – revolver – term loan – bullet – security – charge – defaults – fixed – floating – enforce its security – guarantees – operating company – holding company – parent company guarantee – comfort letter – debenture – syndicated loan – acquisition finance – leveraged buy out (LBO) – highly geared – hedging – derivatives – option – forward – future – interest-rate swap – unwind – currency swap – audit – interim – creditors – debtors – institutional investors – gross margin – operating margin – cash conversion – interest cover – price/earnings ratio – net present value – key performance indicators (KPIs) – balanced scorecard

The best description I've come across about the role of money in business was from a CEO who said it was about 'keeping score'.

Money isn't the reason for doing what you do, but it tells you how well you are doing it.

And the key to this is a company's accounts.

The best business leaders have a facility with numbers. They can read a set of accounts the way an orchestra's conductor can read a music score. Unless you're going to be an accountant you don't need to be as adept. But it helps to know a bit so that when you're in a business meeting – as you will be in due course – you can follow what the people round the table are talking about.

Income Statement And Balance Sheet

The two sets of figures that form a company's accounts are the income statement and the balance sheet.

The **income statement** is what it says it is. It's a record of how much money has come into and gone out of the business over a period. Usually businesses work on a quarterly basis. The quarters are designated Q1, Q2, Q3, Q4 because a company's financial year doesn't have to run from January to December (in fact the tax year in the UK runs from 6 April to 5 April which is weird). So Q1 is the first three months of the company's financial year (whichever calendar months those happen to be) and so on. However, the formal document known as an income statement tends to be for the period of a year (from the start of Q1 to the end of Q4).

The income statements used to be called the **profit and loss account** and is still sometimes referred to as the **P&L**.

You can probably see why businesses have income statements. But what's the purpose of the balance sheet?

The income statement doesn't tell you the whole story. It doesn't tell you how much money is invested in the business (and what assets it is invested in) to generate that income.

The document that does this is the **balance sheet** (it balances assets on the one hand against liabilities on the other). The balance sheet is also prepared once a year.

The fundamental difference between them is this: the income statement is over a period; but the balance sheet is as of a specific date. The balance sheet is a snapshot of the business on that stated date (this date is usually the last day of the business's financial year).

We are going to start with the balance sheet because it's a business's assets that produce sales, and it's the sales that produce profit. The way to think of it is that the company's capital funds its assets. The assets enable the business to do what it does and make sales. And the sales generate the profit.

Balance Sheet In Detail

Almost all businesses have assets of some sort without which they cannot function. A factory needs plant and equipment. A delivery business needs vans. A baker needs an oven. And so on. These assets need to be funded (paid for) in some way. A business's capital requirement is the long-term capital needed to support (pay for) these assets.

Remember, when we looked at setting up a business, how we looked at attracting investors to provide equity funding and we also went to the bank for a loan?

Well, this is the capital supporting the business. It hasn't disappeared. It's just been used to buy assets without which the business wouldn't be able to function.

This money has come from investors and lenders so in a sense it is 'owed' to them. It represents the business's liabilities to them. The assets the money has been used to buy are on the other side of the equation. One equals the other. They balance each other. Hence balance sheet.

The balance sheet sets out the capital invested in my business without which I wouldn't be able to trade at all.

This money is called capital to distinguish it from income. Income happens on a daily basis. Capital is long-term and infrequent.

The balance sheet balances the assets against liabilities. The assets, which are used in the business, consist of **fixed assets** and **current assets**.

Fixed assets don't get consumed. They include the premises, plant and machinery and vehicles.

The current assets do get consumed. They include raw materials (to be manufactured), finished products (to be sold) and cash in the bank (to be spent) as well as money owed by customers (known as trade debtors).

The liabilities fund the assets. They include current liabilities such as overdrafts, short-term borrowings and credit from suppliers (called trade creditors); long-term liabilities such as bank loans and bonds; shareholders' equity invested in the business; and retained profit – profit from previous years that wasn't paid out to shareholders by way of dividend but has been kept (retained) and reinvested in the business. These **retained earnings** become part of a company's capital (additional funding) and liabilities (its prior profit owed to shareholders).

So let's see how a basic balance sheet does it:

Capital and liabilities	£m	Assets	£m
Issued share capital	15	Fixed assets	
		Land / buildings	9
		Machinery / equipment	6
Loan from bank	5	Current assets	
Current liabilities		Raw materials	2
Creditors	2	Finished products	3
		Current debtors	1
		Cash	1
	22		22

A business's balance sheet can tell us a lot about that business. For a start it can tell us how much money the company is making from its assets and how much of the capital (money in the business) is debt and how much is equity. Too much debt and the business can look risky.

If you know what different businesses are using by way of capital you can compare their profitability. If one business makes twice the profit of another but only needs a little more capital to support it, you can tell that it provides a better return on capital (often called **return on capital employed** or **ROCE**). Return on capital is important to investors. They invest capital in order to generate a return on the money they've invested.

In weighing up strategic options, businesses will look at the **ROI** (**return on investment**) of a proposed project: what will we get back if we invest that much money in this project? ROCE does this for the business as a whole.

These are all ways of assessing how well a business is doing and of comparing it to others.

Goodwill As A Balance Sheet Item

An accounting term that affects the balance sheet is 'goodwill'. Goodwill is often included in balance sheets on the right hand side as a fixed asset. It generally means that bit of a business which represents why customers come to it (its reputation) that isn't just a matter of its fixed assets.

It is often used where a company has taken over another and has paid more than the target's actual assets are worth. The excess represents goodwill – that is, the worth of the target over and above the assets it owned.

Goodwill appears under the 'fixed assets' heading – even though it's invisible and you can't see it – and is used to make the company's capital side and assets side balance. One way of looking at goodwill is as part of a business's brand – the intangible reason why customers come to it.

Now let's look at the income statement.

Income Statement

At one level this is easy. Profit is what's left over after you've paid all your expenses. In other words: income less outgoings. Income is what a business earns on a day-to-day basis from trading. It's also called 'sales' or 'gross revenue' or 'turnover'.

Gross profit is the total value of sales less the cost of the products sold. It tells us at the very least whether we are selling goods at a higher figure than they are costing us to make. But it doesn't tell the whole story.

We need to take into account our 'operating expenses' without which we couldn't make the sales. So, for example, costs of distribution; costs of the sales team. After these have been deducted from gross profit what we are left with is 'operating profit'. From this we deduct the funding costs of the business such as interest on loans, to leave profit before tax or **net profit** or net revenue, 'net' meaning after deduction of outgoings.

Profit at a micro level is called **margin** – it's the profit you make per unit of production after deducting the cost of the raw materials and manufacturing that go into the finished product. 'Gross profit' as a percentage of sales is called 'gross margin'.

Some costs are **fixed costs** – the business has them however busy it is and they tend to be long-term (often called **overheads**); whereas others vary in line with how busy the business is and are **variable costs**.

Expenditure	£m	Income	£m
Fixed costs		Revenue from sales	??
Rent	1		
Salaries	8		
Interest paid to bank	2		

Variable costs			
Raw materials	15		
Electricity	2		
Phone bill	1		
	29		??

You'll see that it isn't complete. We know the outgoings for the period were £29 million. If the revenue was more than that, we have made a profit; if less, a loss.

A profit….

Expenditure	£m	Income	£m
Fixed costs		Revenue from sales	32
Rent	1		
Salaries	8		
Interest paid to bank	2		
Variable costs			
Raw materials	15		
Electricity	2		
Phone bill	1		
Net profit	3		
	32		32

…. or a loss

Expenditure	£m	Income	£m
Fixed costs		Revenue from sales	26
Rent	1		
Salaries	8		
Interest paid to bank	2		

Variable costs
  Raw materials
  Electricity
  Phone bill
	15
	2
	1		

		Net profit / loss	(3)
	29		29

We put the profit or loss figure on whichever side it needs to go in order to make the two columns add up (there's an accounting convention that a loss is stated in brackets as above).

You can probably see now that the colloquial expression 'top line' means a company's sales (gross turnover) before taking any costs into account whereas the 'bottom line' means net profit or profit after all outgoings have been deducted.

Depreciation And Amortisation

There are places where the balance sheet and income statement interact.

For instance, the assets employed in the business are ageing. Every year they suffer more wear and tear and will in due course need to be replaced. This cost to the business needs to be captured somewhere and set against the business's profit.

After all, this wear-and-tear is part of the cost of generating the profit. It is called **depreciation** as an asset depreciates – goes down in value – over its useful economic life. So depreciation is about reducing the value of the assets in the business year by year to reflect wear and tear so that when they need to be replaced the money has been set aside to do so.

Depreciation is a cost to the business so is 'expensed' in the income statement.

But, of course, it isn't actually cash going out of the business. It's more an allowance for future expenditure when those assets need replacing. So it's said to be a non-cash expense. It's a sort of reserve for when the asset has to be replaced.

So each year the company allows a bit for depreciation to reflect the fact that sooner or later the equipment will wear out and money will need to be spent replacing it.

As an expense of the business it appears on the left hand side of the income statement, so reduces the profit or increases the loss.

Expenditure	£m	Income	£m
Fixed costs		Revenue from sales	32
Rent	1		
Salaries	8		
Interest paid to bank	2		
Depreciation allowance	1		
Variable costs			
Raw materials	15		
Electricity	2		
Phone bill	1		
Net profit	2		
	32		32

A similar accounting convention is called amortisation. The debt that is helping to support the business and its assets will need to be repaid at some point. **Amortisation** reduces the amount of the debt (notionally) over its life so that by the time the business has to repay it, the debt has been fully allowed for.

When a business borrows money the loan may be for several years. So the repayment of the loan will be split up across the years (amortised). This is a way of ensuring that the business sets aside a bit of money each year to ensure it can pay the amount of the loan in full in the year in which it has to be repaid.

When Profit Is Real

Profit is not always what you think it is.

To you and me, profit is how much cash we have left once our expenses have been paid. But some profit doesn't get turned into cash – at least for a while.

A property company may own lots of properties. It's not proposing to sell them but a value needs to be put on them annually so that the property company itself can be valued and its balance sheet drawn up. For this reason, property companies regularly revalue their property holdings. If these have gone up in value they have made a profit – the difference between the old (lower) valuation and the new (higher) one. If their overall value goes up from one year to the next the company has made a profit. But this profit isn't in cash.

Profit is not the same as cash. The holdings are still exactly the same. They haven't generated any additional cash and, in fact, if property values subsequently fall, it may never be realised.

What about a business that has entered into a long-term contract? At what point does it include the profit from the contract in its accounts? If it does so at the start, then it has booked all of the profit but none of the cost. If at the end, then it has incurred all of the cost before showing any of the profit.

This is why a distinction is drawn between 'profit' and 'cash profit'.

Cash profit is more formally called **ebitda** (earnings before interest, tax, depreciation and amortisation – all of which you now understand). The 'ebit' bit is earnings before interest and tax and is also known as 'operating profit'. Adding depreciation and amortisation back in makes it 'ebitda'.

The key question is how much of the notional profit is turned into actual cash.

This may depend in part on how quickly you get paid. Do you account for the profit when you do the deal or only when the money comes in? If your deals take many years to complete and you account for the profit upfront the business may seem more profitable and cash rich than it actually is. By contrast a business that takes payment upfront before providing the goods or services (think of tickets to music events) may have cash profit of over 100%.

Hence the importance of the cash flow statement.

Cash Flow Statement

This is the missing bit of the jigsaw. The income statement is about profit or loss. The balance sheet is about the capital in the business and its assets.

The **cash flow statement** shows how actual money has been flowing around the business.

It sets out how the cash (or overdraft) position of the business changed over the previous year. It is only historic but it may indicate a pattern.

When a private company lists on the stock exchange one of the financial documents it is required to produce is an 18-month cash flow projection. This is to reassure prospective investors that the business won't run out of cash in the short- to medium-term.

The cash flow statement is an ongoing annual requirement.

Working Capital Requirement

Often a business will borrow money from a bank to fund its cash flow gap (the difference between its day-to-day gross income and outgoings). It's this funding 'gap' that is a business's **working capital requirement**.

Although it's called a 'requirement' it's not a rule as such or required by law. It's simply a statement of the cash flow gap and will differ from business to business. It's a reflection of how well a business manages its income (including debtors) and its outgoings.

For non-accountants the term 'working capital requirement' can be quite confusing. 'Capital' is what I think of as the long-term money underpinning the business (the capital employed in the business) not the money washing through it. But at least the word 'working' is helpful in suggesting it's an everyday matter of cash flow management rather than a long-term capital requirement of the business.

Don't confuse 'working capital requirement' with 'capital requirement'. This latter is about the other aspect of looking at a business's financials: the assets needed in the business and the capital needed to pay for them.

Factoring

One way of helping cash flow is **factoring** (also known as **invoice discounting** or **supply chain finance**). Companies can often wait a long time to get paid. Factoring is where a company sells what it is owed (its **receivables**) to a bank. The bank will pay the company the bulk of what it is owed (say 90%) and keep the rest (here 10%) as its fee for chasing up the debts and waiting for payment. A lot of businesses use factoring – it's a specialist area of banking in its own right.

Asset Finance

Because buying a piece of plant or equipment can be a drain on cash flow, companies may buy equipment by instalments through **hire purchase** or **conditional sale**. They may also just lease it through **asset finance** (also called **finance leasing**) where the bank will buy the asset and lease it (lend it) to the company for the company to use in its business. Asset finance tends to be tax efficient because government provides tax allowances to encourage industry to reinvest in new equipment and so remain competitive.

Loans, Guarantees, Comfort Letters And Derivatives

Other financial terms that may be noted in a company's accounts include the following.

In terms of debt, there are different types of loan:

- A **revolving credit facility** is like an overdraft. With an overdraft there is a maximum up to which you can borrow, but whatever you pay back you can borrow again. So if I have an overdraft facility of £100 at the bank, I can borrow, say, £70, repay £50 and still borrow a further £80. This type of corporate overdraft is often called a **revolver**.
- A **term loan** is a loan for a fixed period. If the company is due to repay the principal all in one go it is said to have a **bullet** repayment (unlike, say, a repayment mortgage where the monthly payments include interest and a bit of principal, so that by the end of the mortgage all of the principal has been paid off as well as the interest on it).

A lending bank may require a company to provide **security** – that is, a legal mechanism (often called a **charge**) that allows the bank to seize and sell the company's assets if the company **defaults** (fails to repay interest or principal) so that the bank can recover what it is owed. A charge may be **fixed** (over particular assets) or **floating** (which allows the company to buy or sell those assets). If the bank seizes and sells the company's assets it is said to **enforce its security**.

Banks may also seek **guarantees** that the borrower will repay. So, for example, a bank may lend to an **operating company** in a group (a company that carries on part of the group's business) but may seek a guarantee from the **holding company** (the top company) in the group. This is often called a **parent company guarantee** (because the holding company is the parent of all the others in the group, which are its subsidiaries). An assurance that falls short of an outright guarantee is called a **comfort letter** (to give the bank 'comfort' that the parent company won't allow its operating company or subsidiary to become insolvent).

A **debenture** is a type of debt security issued by a public company.

If a company wants to borrow more than one bank is prepared to lend (because the size of the loan will expose the bank to too much of the borrower's risk) the bank may bring in a syndicate (pool) of other banks to lend to the borrower on the same terms. This is called a **syndicated loan**. There is one loan agreement and all the banks sign it. One use of syndicated loans is in M&A transactions, where bank lending is called **acquisition finance**.

An acquisition which uses a very high level of debt is often called an **LBO** (**leveraged buy out** where 'leveraged' means **highly geared**, that is, a lot of debt in proportion to equity).

Hedging is about reducing risk through the use of financial instruments called **derivatives** (because they are derived from other financial instruments or transactions).

There are three types of derivative: options, futures (also called forwards) and swaps.

An **option** enables a company to fix a price at which to buy or sell something in case that price starts to change. So an airline may take out an option to buy aviation fuel at a specific price if it is worried that the price may have increased by the time it comes to need the fuel.

Alternatively it may decide to buy the fuel at today's price for delivery in, say, six months' time when it will need it. This is called a **forward** and, if it is an instrument that you can trade on an exchange, it is called a **future**.

An **interest-rate swap** enables a company that has one type of interest rate (say, fixed) to swap it for another (say, variable) – which it may want to do if it thinks interest rates are going down but it doesn't want to **unwind** the loan completely (because doing so would be more expensive than entering into the swap). A **currency swap** enables a company to swap one currency for another which a multinational operating in many countries may want to do.

These are all financial terms you may come across in the notes to a company's accounts.

Annual Audit

Public companies are required to have an annual **audit** in which the auditors (external accountants) state that the accounts (income statement and balance sheet) present 'a true and fair view' of the business.

Public companies also provide **interim** figures on a quarterly basis. They are called quarterly because they cover the previous three months and they are interim because they provide a less detailed overview (a stop-gap) till the next annual accounts.

A company's accounts are public records so that **creditors** (those owed money by the company) can see how creditworthy it is (by contrast, **debtors** owe the company money, such as customers who have yet to pay).

Creditors will be concerned with a company's ability to pay them. They will focus on cash flow and profitability. If a company has strong cash flow and is profitable it is a good credit risk.

For their part, the shareholders want to know how their business is doing (as do potential investors who are weighing up whether to buy shares in it or not).

Institutional Investors

The biggest investors are called **institutional investors**. They are insurance companies, pension funds and fund managers. They get the money to invest from us, you and me.

When we take out insurance, the premium we pay is invested by the insurance company in the market. Out of the investment return it meets any claims and makes a profit.

When we are in work we pay into a pension fund for when we retire. That money is invested in the market over our working life to produce a pot of money for us to live on in retirement (state pensions don't work like this – they are paid out of the government's current tax income and so are said to be 'unfunded').

If you have enough money to save or invest you might put it into a tax-free wrapper, for a fund manager to invest in the market for you.

So all these institutional investors, ultimately, get their money from us. But from so many of us that in their hands it becomes a mountain of money to invest, which is why they are very big institutions.

How Investors Analyse Companies

Investors want to know whether a company is worth investing in. They will look at the following (amongst many) factors, some of which we've already covered:

ROCE (return on capital employed). The balance sheet will give them an idea of this. If a business makes a lot of profit without much need of capital (small balance sheet) it's a better investment prospect than one making the same profit but requiring a lot of capital (big balance sheet).

Gross margin. How much more a company can sell its product for, over the cost of making it. This is sales less cost of sales (the price the customer pays for a product less the cost of making that product). Typically investors will look for gross margin of 60% (a product that customers buy for £10 costs the company £4 to make).

Operating margin. This is the gross margin less the indirect costs such as premises, people, promotion and so on (investors look for 25%).

Cash conversion. This is how much of the earnings (profit on paper) actually gets turned into cash which can be paid to shareholders or invested in the business. Investors look for 90%, comparing the cash flow number and the profit number – 'net' versus 'net' or 'operating' versus 'operating' (so you're comparing like with like). They avoid companies with poor cash conversion – rising profits and deteriorating cash flow is bad news.

Leverage. The level of debt to equity (the lower the better).

Interest cover. By how much the cost of servicing loans is covered by profit (the higher the better).

If a company is worth investing in, the next question is whether its shares are worth buying now. This is a matter of the **price/earnings ratio**. The p/e ratio tells you the cost of the company in terms of the dividend income it produces.

So a company on a p/e of 20 will cost you 20 years of dividends to buy. A company on a p/e of 4 will cost you four years' dividend income. The first is obviously significantly higher than the second but that will be for good reason. For instance, the first may be a rapidly growing company and the second one may be in a mature and possibly declining industry.

Research analysts look at investments in terms of the future return. That future return is then discounted back (reduced) to the present to give a current value (a value you can put on it now). This gives you what is called the **net present value**. NPV calculations are common in business. They are part of the ROI assessment of a proposed strategic project.

The Limitation Of Accounts

Accounts don't present a single, definitive image of how well a business is doing. Instead they paint a series of pictures, of interpretations. Numbers can never provide a perfect scientific analysis. A business is dynamic and forward-looking. Accounts are historic and backward-looking. This is why accountancy is not about adding up columns of boring figures. It's about interpreting those figures to paint a picture or tell a story.

Within any business there will be some **key performance indicators** (**KPIs**) which are internal measures used to monitor whether the business is on track or not.

There are also other, non-financial factors which are used to gauge the health of an organisation. Kaplan and Norton were two business school academics who developed the **balanced scorecard** which includes financial measures but also cultural indicators of how well a business is doing and is likely to do.

Which is a good point at which to broaden our horizons and look beyond the confines of business.

CHAPTER 5

THE BUSINESS OF GOVERNMENT

Public sector – private sector – third sector – non-governmental organisations (NGOs) – not-for-profits – communist economies – capitalist economies – nationalisation – privatisation – global initial public offering – commercialisation – franchise – concession – trade sale – public private partnership (PPP) – private finance initiative (PFI) – off balance sheet (OBS) – monopolies – regulator – cartels – competition authority – market dominant – antitrust – regulation – finance leasing – asset finance – gross domestic product (GDP) – balance of payments – public sector borrowing requirement (PSBR) – run on the bank – interest rates – inflation – demand – supply – real value – central banks – deflation – corporate responsibility – stakeholders – corporate governance

We need to set business in a wider context. I said at the beginning that business provides us with everything we need. It's not quite true.

There are big things such as 'peace', 'security', 'education' and 'health' that are provided by government, along with clean streets and refuse collection (the latter provided by local government). The government (central and local) is called the **public sector**. Business is called the **private sector**.

There are sectors that in some countries are state-owned (and are part of the public sector) and in others are private, such as transport (trains, airlines, airports and ports), utilities and energy (water, electricity, gas, oil), broadcasting (TV and radio) and telecoms (phones).

Confusingly the term 'public' is used to describe public companies, listed on stock exchanges (where the public can buy their shares) as well as the 'public sector'. Public companies are very much part of the private sector.

Government is there to serve and protect us, the citizens. But it, too, has to be business-like. Government departments and local authorities have to have business plans, they have budgets to work to, and they need to cut out waste by being efficient. So they may not be there to make a profit, but they certainly don't want to make losses and they generally operate along business lines.

In addition there is the not-for-profit sector also known as the **third sector** or the third way. The third sector includes charities, educational bodies and other **non-governmental organisations** (**NGOs**) that seek to do good in the world. They are generally known as **not-for-profits** but they too need to be business-like. Charities need to raise money from donors and be careful how they spend it. Otherwise, if they are wasteful, their funding will be cut and their donors will desert them.

The boundary between the public and private sectors is fuzzy and subject to constant change. There are public sector services that are delivered in part by or in conjunction with the private sector. Peace and security depend in part on the defence industry. Education includes private schools and colleges. Health includes pharmaceutical companies, private hospitals and providers of health insurance.

In **communist economies** the idea is that the state owns everything including (as Karl Marx put it) the means of production and provides everything we need. There is no profit motive as such and no competition: there's no need for either. In **capitalist economies** capital (money) is channelled to those businesses that can put it to best use. Their reward is profit which they use to re-invest to expand and to reward their investors.

Which is better? That's a question for politicians and political scientists. However, it may be that countries need different systems at different stages of their development.

A very poor country dependent on an agrarian (agricultural) economy with very little by way of infrastructure (roads, schools, hospitals) may be better off as a communist state so that everyone gets a bit of everything (food, clothing, healthcare, education).

A developed economy is better off with capitalism which encourages innovation and change. Capitalism allows people to harness their own energy and enthusiasm for their own reward. The challenge is to make sure that others less able or fortunate aren't left behind: a ladder for those who can climb up and a safety net for those who can't.

Over the last hundred years there has been a trend for communist states to begin to embrace capitalism and for capitalist countries to move even more business from the public to the private sectors.

In fact whole industries can move between the two.

Nationalisation

Nationalisation occurs when a government takes a private sector enterprise into public (state) ownership. Some industries – such as defence – are usually regarded as so critical to national security that they will always remain in public ownership, meaning that the government owns them. In some countries this extends to arms manufacture, electricity generation and so on.

Sometimes nationalisation is the result of a financial crisis: many banks were nationalised in the global financial crisis because they would otherwise have gone bust.

Privatisation

Privatisation is where an entire state-owned industry, often a monopoly, is moved into the private sector by turning it into a business with owners and customers. Privatisation has been used in virtually all sectors, from energy production and transmission (oil, gas and electricity, for example), utilities (such as water), transport (railways, airlines, airports, roads, bridges and ports) to mineral and other resource extraction, industrial plant projects, waste treatment processes and financial services.

By attracting private sector investment, these old state enterprises can modernise more quickly and improve the services they offer consumers, often in newly-opened up competitive markets that offer consumers lower prices.

Commercialisation

There are different types of privatisation. At its purest and grandest, it is about selling off state-owned industries often in their entirety – for instance through a **global initial public offering** where shares in the industry are offered around the world to investors.

But less extreme versions include **commercialisation** (subjecting an activity to private sector competition, which may include joint ventures between the state and the private sector), the grant of a **franchise** or **concession** (allowing the private sector to offer that service) or a **trade sale** (selling the industry to a private-sector entity already in that business). All of these cases may be accompanied by **market liberalisation** (removing state controls so anyone can compete).

PPP And PFI

Sometimes government will look to the private sector for involvement or financing in big infrastructure projects (like roads, railways, hospitals, power stations) which government lacks the expertise to build or fund alone.

This can be undertaken through **public private partnership** (**PPP**) or **private finance initiative** (**PFI**) transactions. For example, a private contractor may build a road and be allowed by government to charge users a toll (a fee) for using it. Out of this the contractor recovers the cost of building the road plus a profit but with the agreement that after, say, thirty years, the road reverts to public ownership and the government takes it over.

Off Balance Sheet

Governments also use **off balance sheet** (**OBS**) finance to fund long-term projects. OBS has come in for criticism as a way of hiding a company's liabilities away from its accounts (the balance sheet in particular). But the reason why government uses it is because government's money is all income (taxes and borrowing). It doesn't have capital saved up.

So using income to fund long-term projects, whose benefit will be felt over many years and which may not come on-stream for several, distorts a government's finances. It may look spendthrift when in fact it is using its current account to fund long-term beneficial improvements to society. OBS finance enables it to undertake such projects without distorting its current income and outgoings.

Competition And Regulation

Many state-owned industries are **monopolies** (there is only one provider). So when they are privatised competition has to be introduced, by encouraging multiple providers and introducing a government **regulator** that polices prices.

This is because monopolies can lead to inefficiency, poor innovation, poor investment and high prices to consumers.

So the state becomes involved with the private sector in another way – through competition and regulation. For instance, the state will ban **cartels** (a cartel is a group of companies working together to fix prices) and will set up a **competition authority** that enforces laws preventing businesses from becoming **market dominant** or gaining monopoly advantage. Many M&A deals get referred to national competition authorities for this reason. In the US competition law is called **antitrust** (from the days when cartels in the US were called 'trusts').

Competition law is a form of **regulation** designed to protect the consumer. But the state regulates business in other ways, for instance in preventing pharmaceuticals from being sold without proper testing and licensing, or ensuring that foodstuffs are properly labelled with their ingredients and are date-stamped.

Government Incentives For Business

The state also encourages business by providing tax incentives for investment, regional grants to encourage businesses to open factories in areas of economic deprivation and free-trade zones to encourage international trade.

For example, governments may use tax reliefs to encourage companies to invest in new plant and machinery (this is the basis of **finance leasing**, also called **asset finance**, mentioned earlier). This is to ensure that business remains efficient and competitive.

Governments recognise that companies (which make up a country's private sector) are the principal contributor to a country's economic prosperity. Companies pay corporation tax (taxes companies pay government out of their profits) which provides government with income. They also provide employment: people in work do not need to be supported by the state and they also pay taxes to the state out of their earnings and local taxes (council tax) to the local authority where they live.

So the private sector provides government – central and local – with its income. Some politicians (on all sides) would do well to remember that without a vibrant private sector there would be no economy and very little money for government to spend and spread around.

Governments look closely at their country's **GDP** (**gross domestic product**) which measures annual output in goods and services. This is broken down into private and government consumption, investment and exports (known as the **balance of payments** – if they are positive it means the country is exporting more than it's importing; if not, the country is consuming more than it is producing).

So the relationship between business and government is symbiotic (interdependent).

Running The Public And Third Sectors Like Businesses

There is another way in which the public and private sectors interact, and that is that the public sector is itself becoming more business-minded. Government has only two sources of income to run the country: taxes and borrowing. If a government taxes its citizenry too highly it will be voted out of office. Whatever it borrows has to be repaid (known as the **public sector borrowing requirement** or **PSBR**). So government has become more commercial in its outlook.

This is why, even if you want to be a teacher or a health worker or work in the police service, you will need to be commercially aware, in order to do more with less resource.

The same is true of the third sector. Charities are funded by public donations. The people leading them have to be commercially aware in order to make the most of those donations. The third sector is run along business lines too.

The Role Of The Central Bank

There is a direct way in which government impacts the economy and business, and this is through the setting of interest rates.

Interest rates are set by a country's central bank. The central bank is part of the state but separate from government. Its job is to set interest rates, control the country's money supply (part of this job is printing a country's currency) and regulate a country's banks.

The central bank is sometimes called 'the lender of last resort' because it bails out banks that are at risk of going bust. We wouldn't leave our money in banks if there was a risk we wouldn't get it back. So governments guarantee depositors' money and this prevents **a run on the bank** (panic withdrawals) as it's called. Our money doesn't lie around in banks doing nothing. Instead banks lend it out to businesses which use the money to expand.

Interest Rates And How They Move

Governments (through their central banks) use **interest rates** to control inflation.

Inflation is prices going up. When an economy is doing well, people earn more and spend more. This increases **demand** for goods and services and causes prices to increase while the **supply** of those goods and services catches up (supply and demand are technical terms in economics).

Inflation erodes the **real value** of money. 'Real value' is what money actually buys you. If prices go up your money will buy you less. Its real value has been eroded.

Governments generally don't like inflation. Those most affected (the poor, those on benefit and the elderly) are on low or fixed incomes and if they are squeezed too much will look to government to bail them out. This costs governments money. And if inflation becomes extreme it can destroy confidence in the currency and the economy.

The only way to control inflation is to stop people spending so much – either by raising taxes (which makes government unpopular) or by increasing the cost of borrowing so they borrow and spend less.

Central banks increase the cost of borrowing by increasing interest rates. 'Base rate' is the rate that (in the UK) the government pays to borrow.

To raise interest rates the Bank of England (the UK's central bank) issues new government bonds for sale (UK government bonds are called 'gilts' from when they had a silver edge). These gilts will pay the new (higher) base rate so investors will buy them. The money that investors pay to the Bank for the gilts is taken out of circulation. The money supply shrinks. Money becomes tighter. Inflation declines.

But increasing interest rates too rapidly chokes off lending, stunts economic growth and can plunge a country into recession (defined as six months of declining growth). It can lead to **deflation**. Here, people don't spend because they know the price of goods and services will be cheaper tomorrow – but then they don't buy them tomorrow either, because prices will be lower still the following day. So demand dries up, industry falters and the economy grinds to a halt.

To avoid this, in order to lower interest rates and stimulate the economy, the Bank will buy the gilts that are paying the highest rate of interest. This withdraws that tranche of gilts from the market leaving lower-paying gilts, whose rate then becomes the new base rate. The money the Bank spends to buy these higher-paying gilts enters the money supply, increasing it. People can borrow at a lower interest rate, borrow more cheaply, borrow more and spend more.

Let's just go through the knock-on effects of an increase in interest rates. When interest rates go up:

The stock market goes down. This happens for two reasons. The cost of borrowing goes up, so company profits will go down, so investors sell shares. And money that would have gone into the stock market instead is put on deposit at banks because they are now paying a higher, more attractive rate of interest.

The pound sterling goes up. The increase in interest rates makes the UK a more attractive destination for international investors' cash. But to put their money on deposit at UK banks they need to translate that money into sterling (the pound). This demand for sterling increases its value against other currencies.

UK exports go down. When sterling goes up it makes the cost of goods and services that the UK sells internationally more expensive for buyers in other countries (using their own currency) to buy. And it reduces profits earned in other currencies (overseas earnings) because they buy less sterling when repatriated.

These linkages, between interest rates, the stock market, the currency, exports, cost of borrowing and company profits work in reverse too.

If interest rates come down (to boost the economy through monetary loosening), bank deposits become less attractive (they pay less interest). Sterling weakens so UK exporters sell more goods and services. The stock market goes up because companies that borrow (most of them) will now make more profit, as will exporters.

If the Bank of England has been signalling for some time that interest rates are likely to rise then, when it happens, the market may not move much at all. This is because everyone was expecting it so that the news has already been 'discounted in the price' as the market puts it. In fact if the economy is overheating and policy makers don't take corrective action the market may panic if it thinks the economy is out of control and the policy makers don't know what they're doing.

This is what market professionals mean by 'market confidence': confidence that policy makers know what they are doing and are going to do it.

Corporate Citizenship

A final point on the role of business in society: businesses are increasingly aware of their responsibilities towards the wider community and the planet.

Corporate responsibility (also known as corporate citizenship) is the idea that a business is not there just to make money but owes a duty to its **stakeholders**, such as its employees and their families, pensioners (past employees), its local community and its customers, as well as its owners. It also owes a duty to the environment hence the emphasis on green energy and reducing the carbon footprint. This social awareness extends to encouraging a diverse workforce which is representative of society in terms of gender, religion and ethnicity.

A specific aspect of this is **corporate governance** which is about how a business is made accountable to its owners and stakeholders.

We've looked at business in a wider context. Now it's time to do the opposite – to go inside a business and see what it looks like from within.

CHAPTER 6

HOW ORGANISATIONS ARE ORGANISED

Functions – chief executive officer (CEO) – board of directors – chairman – non-executive directors – remuneration committee – business schools – chief operating officer (COO) – line manager – appraisal – chief financial officer (CFO) – finance director (FD) – treasury – business development – sales – marketing – brand management – corporate identity – production – just-in-time – continuous improvement – quality movement – procurement – logistics – supply chain management – manufacturing economy – service economy – trade marks – copyright – patents – portfolio – intellectual property rights (IPR) – chief information officer (CIO) – research & development (R&D) – human resources – learning & development (L&D) – facilities management – back office – cost centres – profit centre – enterprise resource planning (ERP) – best-in-class – risk management – in-house legal function – insurance – health & safety – reputational risk – organisational design – outsource – service level agreements (SLAs) – professional service firms (PSFs) – accountants – audit – auditors – reporting accountants – corporate finance – tax advisers – bankers – brokers – fund managers – actuaries – host company – plan sponsor – insurance brokers – insureds – loss adjusters – key man insurance – media and advertising agencies – account managers – copywriters – graphic designers – media buyers – digital agencies – sales promotion – market research – marketing consultants – PR consultants – public relations – investor relations – lobbyists – public affairs – lawyers – in-house lawyers – legal department – legal executives – paralegals – patent attorneys – property consultants – quantity surveyors – architects – interior designers – engineers – structural engineers – management consultants – legacy systems

When an entrepreneur starts a business it will be little more than an idea on a kitchen table. But as it gets bigger, the entrepreneur will need to bring in more and more people to help.

Initially everyone may do everything. But soon they start to specialise. By the time a company lists on a stock exchange and becomes a public company its **functions** (the corporate name for its internal departments) will be well established.

Business Leadership

At the top of the tree running the company is the **CEO (chief executive officer)** or MD (Managing Director). The CEO or MD is ultimately responsible for how well the company does. If it does badly they tend to go.

The company will also have a **board of directors**. Each director will be responsible for one or more of the company's functions. Their job is to help the CEO. In addition, in the case of public companies, there is likely to be a chairman and some non-executive directors.

The **chairman** of the board is senior to the CEO or MD and tends to have an outward-facing, strategic and ambassadorial role. But it is the chairman who tends to be instrumental in getting rid of the CEO or MD if the latter isn't doing the job well and has lost the confidence of the board.

The **non-executive directors** (who may be CEOs or chairs of other businesses) do not have any direct responsibilities in the business (hence 'non-executive'). But they are invited to join the board because of their business acumen and expertise. They provide additional insight and input when the board meets to discuss the running of the company. They will also tend to run the **remuneration committee** which fixes the pay for the company's senior people (including the CEO).

The role of leadership in a business is subject to intense analysis and discussion at **business schools** and in publications like the *Harvard Business Review*.

Chief Operating Officer

Beneath the CEO in the biggest businesses is the **chief operating officer (COO)**. The COO's role is to look after the business's day-to-day workings. The other directors may report to the COO with a 'dotted-line' report to the CEO.

'Report' is the business term for who your boss is. Your boss is also called your **line manager**. A dotted-line report means that you need to tell that person what you are doing but they are not your line manager. Your line manager sets your pay, gives you your objectives and tells you how you are doing (which is called your **appraisal**). They are responsible for 'hiring and firing' (bringing people in and if necessary letting them go). The term 'dotted line' comes from organisational charts ('organograms') of how businesses are organised which show direct reports to line managers as unbroken lines and indirect reports as dotted lines.

Chief Financial Officer

Whether or not a business has a COO, the next most important member of the board after the CEO is the **CFO** (**chief financial officer**), also known as the **finance director** or **FD**. He or she is in control of the money side of the business. This embraces how the business is funded and what it does with excess cash (known as **treasury**), how quickly money is collected from customers (Accounts Receivable) and how suppliers are paid (Accounts Payable). The finance function is responsible for the company's accounts and deals with external auditors. It may also have a tax team that oversees the company's annual corporate tax return and how much the company pays in tax.

Business Development

In any business there will be a **business development** function, which is about getting and keeping customers. In a manufacturing company this may be called 'Sales & Marketing'. You'll remember that **sales** is the sharp end of converting possible customers into actual ones while **marketing** is wider: it's about how a business positions itself and its products to appeal to the market more generally.

However, the whole issue of how a business presents itself and its products to the market has become wider. It includes **brand management** (the products that customers see) and **corporate identity** (how the company portrays itself including its slogans and logos) as well as reputation management and public relations (what a company says about itself and its products). PR has itself expanded over the years to include investor relations (addressing the company's shareholders) and public affairs (addressing government, also known as lobbying).

Production

If the company is a manufacturer of goods rather than a provider of services, a key function will be **Production**. This is much more than just making the goods. It's about ensuring that production isn't interrupted.

Companies are always looking for ways to cut costs and improve efficiency by improving their processes (the way they do things). This has led to waves of production innovation including just-in-time production and continuous improvement (also known as kaizen), both of which were developed in Japan.

With **just-in-time** production you don't hold big inventories of stock (which would be a drain on cash flow) – instead you have only what you need immediately to hand. However, you have to have slick processes to ensure you have all the materials you need at the right time. Any breakdown costs a company a lot in terms of lost production – units that should have been made but weren't. **Continuous improvement** is about constantly questioning how and why you do things in order to improve your processes and make them more efficient.

Both are examples of the **quality movement** in industry. Quality here is a technical term. It means driving out faulty manufacturing through statistical analysis so that almost no defective products are ever made. The modern example is Six Sigma – a productivity-enhancement programme.

If a business buys in a lot of raw materials (for instance for manufacturing into goods), it will have a **procurement** function in charge of negotiating the best terms and lowest prices.

Logistics Or Supply Chain Management

Once you've made the goods they have to be delivered. This is **logistics** or **supply chain management** – ensuring that transportation is as efficient as possible (trucks don't travel full one way and empty the other) and meeting seasonal demands. Whole books and academic studies are written on the subject.

Chief Information Officer

As the developed world becomes less of a **manufacturing economy** and more of a **service economy**, what a company knows becomes its biggest source of competitive advantage.

In some business sectors, such as pharmaceuticals, biotech and healthcare, a company's most valuable assets can be its **intellectual property** (**IP**) which includes **trade marks** (to protect brands), **copyright** (for instance my copyright in this book as its author) and **patents** (which protect inventions). Some big companies may have a **portfolio** of patents and many registered trade marks. These collections of patents and trade marks are referred to collectively as **intellectual property rights** (**IPR**).

In businesses with important IPR, this function may be led by a **chief information officer** (**CIO**) and may also include a business's technology. In the past technology was headed by a technology director or CTO (chief technology officer) but, as Peter Drucker said, we are now in a knowledge economy so what matters now is less the computer systems a company uses and more what they are used for. The CIO may therefore be responsible for the company's intranet and its knowledge management systems.

Some companies may also have large **Research & Development** (**R&D**) functions developing a pipeline of new products for when the IPR on their current biggest-sellers run out. The R&D function may be separate from the CIO's role because of its importance to the future development of the business (for instance in pharmaceuticals, the R&D function is probably the single most important part of the business – researching and designing future cures which will guarantee the company's future income).

Back Office Functions

Then there are functions common to all businesses. These include, for instance, **human resources** – which used to be called 'Personnel' – which advises on the hiring of staff, their terms and conditions, their pay, their performance **appraisals** and their training (often called **learning & development** or L&D).

Another is **facilities management** which includes everything from running the staff canteen and keeping the toilets clean to making sure everyone has a place to work, operation of the switchboard and delivery of the mail.

These functions are not customer-facing and are known collectively as **back office**. They are **cost centres** whereas anything in the business that makes money is a **profit centre**.

ERP

Many of these back office functions are common to many companies so they can be standardised and automated through **enterprise resource planning** (ERP) which is a software-driven way of achieving lower cost and greater efficiency through having standard processes. These are often called **best-in-class** if they are adopted across a sector.

Risk Management

A more recent function is **risk management**. This has developed rapidly.

Companies started to recruit their own lawyers to reduce the cost of going to outside law firms. This became known as the legal department or **in-house legal function**. It would often take in the company secretarial team (which looks after the business's compliance with company law and regulation).

Then the term 'risk management' came in to address wider risks businesses face, from **insurance** (insuring the company's assets against loss) and **health & safety** (injuries to employees) to **reputational risk** (which overlaps with PR).

Some sectors are highly regulated and the businesses involved may need to be licensed (pharmaceutical companies need licences for their drugs, for example). Maintaining these regulatory approvals – without which a business in a regulated sector cannot function – is a key part of what the risk function addresses. All public companies have to set out in their annual reports the risks they think they face.

Organisational Design

The way a business is organised is itself a management discipline that is studied and taught at business schools. It's called **organisational design**.

Companies are forever assessing what they should keep in-house (as part of their organisation) and what they can put out to external contractors. This can range from upkeep of their technology to catering in staff restaurants and cleaning the rest rooms.

Sometimes they may **outsource** an entire function, that is, contract with an external supplier to provide a service that was previously resourced and delivered in-house. The theory is that the external supplier will deliver a better service (because that is its specialisation) at a lower cost (because it generates economies of scale from providing the same service to many businesses).

These outsourcing arrangements can be set up to last many years. If so, part of the deal may be that the business gets the benefit of advances in the service provided. For instance, an outsourced technology provider may provide updated systems as part of the deal and the business may transfer its own relevant staff to the outsource provider. You can begin to see why outsourcing agreements can be complex. The key elements are **service level agreements (SLAs)**.

Even without going that far and putting an entire function out-of-house, businesses are big users of external professional services. These service providers are called **professional service firms** or **PSFs**. Here are some of the principal types.

Audit And Tax

Accountants First and foremost companies are concerned with numbers – profitability, cash flow, tax and so on. The CFO and the finance function will use a firm of external accountants to do the annual **audit** (a regulatory requirement). We've seen that these figures are what external stakeholders, such as investors, suppliers and creditors, rely on when deciding whether to invest in or do business with the company. A company's **auditors** check the information that goes into the company's annual report and accounts. In the biggest companies, teams of external auditors are at work almost the whole year round. But accountants get involved in other ways. They may be **reporting accountants**, overseeing the financials of a bid, for example. Smaller companies may use accountants for **corporate finance** advice, on the raising of money.

Tax advisers Companies are sensitive about tax because it reduces cash flow and is paid out of profit. The popular image is that companies are unethical and use tax dodges to pay as little tax as possible. While a very small minority of companies may behave like this, by far the majority try to achieve a balance – fulfilling their duty to shareholders to minimise the tax take while complying wholeheartedly with the law. Tax advisers can be lawyers or accountants or members of the CIOT (Chartered Institute of Taxation).

Finance And Pensions

Bankers Most major companies have close relationships with their banks. They will have a commercial bank which arranges loans for them and an investment bank that advises them on issuing bonds and shares. Investment banks also advise on mergers and acquisitions (M&A). Bankers guard their client relationships jealously.

Brokers The term broker means intermediary. For example, a commodity broker sells commodities ('hard' ones include metals; 'soft' ones are agricultural produce). Smaller public companies may not have a lead bank, but they will tend to have a corporate broker, a firm that is a member of the stock exchange on which they are listed and which advises them on share issues. Many brokers are owned by banks.

Fund managers Fund managers are also known as asset managers, investment managers, money managers, portfolio managers and wealth managers. They manage money on behalf of a company's pension fund.

Every major company has a pension fund which provides pensions to employees to live on once they retire. If a pension fund is big enough, it may have its own in-house fund managers employed to invest its money. But most pension funds put at least some of their money out to external asset managers.

Some also use **actuaries**. Actuaries are statisticians who help pension funds work out what their future liabilities are likely to be and then advise them on how to manage their assets to generate a return to meet those liabilities.

A pension fund is separate from its **host company** (also called a **plan sponsor** – 'plan' means a pension fund). It is run by trustees who owe a duty to present and future members. Fund managers report on a quarterly basis to a pension fund's trustees. Those who persistently underperform are replaced.

Insurance brokers Insurance is a major concern for companies. It protects them against all sorts of catastrophes and systems failures that could disrupt and even destroy the business. Insurance brokers act as intermediaries between **insureds** (companies) and insurance companies, helping insureds buy insurance cover as cheaply as possible and advising on the sort of cover most appropriate. **Loss adjusters** will assess the value of a claim and negotiate a settlement between the insured and the insurance company. Some big companies choose to 'self insure' (which means 'not insure'). In other words they bear any loss themselves on the basis that this works out more cheaply over the longer term if they are keeping the premium they would otherwise be paying. Insurers are institutional investors and can be extremely large and international in their own right. Major companies tend to have **key man insurance** which protects them against the loss through illness or otherwise of senior staff without whom their business would be seriously impaired.

Brand Development And Protection

Media and advertising agencies There are media agencies that specialise in helping companies build and protect their brands, advertise and generate sales.

All major companies that sell goods and services B2C use all sorts of media to reach their consumers. Traditionally they would advertise on television, newspapers, billboards and in public places (trains and buses, for instance).

Advertising agencies remain the biggest media agencies. They have **account managers** who deal with their clients, **copywriters** who write the words ('copy' here means a piece of text), **graphic designers** to produce the artwork and **media buyers** who book space where the adverts will be displayed or shown. Some advertising agencies have become enormous global corporations. But traditional advertising is in retreat now that **digital agencies** advise companies specifically on how to use the internet and social media to reach markets.

There are media agencies that advise companies on image and brand management and are involved at a strategic level in helping to define a business and its markets and what it says about itself. More routinely they develop new logos. **Sales promotion** agencies focus on the point-of-sale, such as promotions in stores and special offers using eye-catching displays, freebies and competitions. **Market research** agencies talk to businesses and consumers to find out what they want or their attitude to a proposed product. They provide detailed data on actual and potential markets.

There are all sorts of other **marketing consultants**, from those collecting data to do market segmentation (dividing the market up into types of customer to target) to those offering databases and systems to collate customer information. Others specialise in helping companies make tenders for big contracts. Still others provide training to staff in business development skills.

Marketing specialists talk about 'above the line' and 'below the line'. Above the line includes advertising. Below the line includes sales promotion.

PR consultants Over the past 20 years **public relations** (originally 'press relations') has become a specialist part of marketing in its own right. PR agencies put out press releases for clients, get articles 'placed' in the press, train clients in media skills (how to answer tricky questions on TV), develop disaster plans and input to image and strategy. Financial PR is heavily involved in M&A activity where takeovers can be won or lost depending on press comment and public perception. **Investor relations** is a part of PR that is specifically about how a public company addresses its shareholders.

Lobbyists This profession is well established in the US but is more recent in the UK although there are several thousand – mainly ex-politicians and civil servants. Their job is to make sure their clients' concerns are raised at the right levels of government (the term 'lobby' comes from the lobbies or hallways in Parliament). Industries that are likely to be affected by legislation and regulation use their trade bodies, advised by lobbyists, to press their case to ensure that they are not too adversely affected. Because of its involvement with government it's often called **public affairs**.

Law

Lawyers All major companies use lawyers. The biggest companies employ their own lawyers, called **in-house lawyers**, who work in the company's **legal department**. But specialist legal work or work requiring a large team may be put out-of-house to external law firms. Lawyers are either solicitors or barristers. Traditionally, barristers appeared in court and solicitors didn't but this distinction is fading. There are lawyers such as **legal executives** and **paralegals** who are less qualified but can provide certain legal services more cheaply.

Lawyers tend to be contentious (dealing with disputes, also known as 'litigation') or non-contentious (doing transactions and giving advice) and they specialise in different areas of law.

Patent attorneys These are part-lawyers, part-scientists and deal with intellectual property. They help companies protect their know-how and inventions by filing for patent registration. Big companies that do a lot of R&D, for instance in sectors like pharmaceuticals and electronics, will have in-house patent attorneys looking after their IP portfolios since these will be a core part of their business and its value. Licensing patents for other companies to use can be big business for companies with extensive IP portfolios. Patent attorneys also advise on copyright and trade marks.

Property

Property consultants All major businesses have premises (including offices, retail outlets, factories and warehouses) and have property consultants to negotiate the terms with their landlords. This is because most businesses do not own their premises. To do so would tie up too much capital and be inflexible if a company wanted to expand or move. Instead companies rent from commercial property landlords which tend to be institutional investors such as insurance companies, pension funds, fund managers and big property companies specialising in development.

Property consultants are usually surveyors, professionals able to value property and negotiate leases. Some of these firms have become big international businesses in their own right, serving their clients' property needs all over the world. They have agency departments that broker deals (acquisition and disposal of land and buildings) and act on behalf of developers acquiring sites for development. They also have advisory practices that help with planning applications and the management of property on behalf of institutional landlords. This includes dealing with corporate tenants, rent reviews and dilapidations (getting tenants to make good any wear and tear).

Quantity surveyors These have nothing to do with surveyors although many belong to the same profession. Quantity surveyors specialise in construction projects. They control the associated costs by undertaking feasibility studies, cost estimating, valuations and cost benefit analysis. They assess the cost of work, labour, materials and plant.

Architects are mainly involved in 'newbuilds' but may be brought in to help a company design additional space. One type are **interior designers** who don't just advise on the colour of furnishings but help companies get the best ergonomical use of their premises ('fitting out' is the term for installing the interiors of a newbuild).

Engineers Also known as 'civil engineers' (the very first engineers were military), they construct buildings, bridges, roads, ports and airports. **Structural engineers** specialise in foundations and how buildings stay up, highway engineers specialise in roads. The term 'engineer' applies more widely beyond construction to ships (marine engineers), aircraft (aviation engineers), cars (automotive engineers), electrical engineers and so on.

Management Consultancy And Technology

Management consultants These form the biggest pool of external advisers and their specialisations extend from strategy and organisational design to HR and training. Increasingly technology is a key focus in all these areas.

Big businesses, especially banks, struggle with **legacy systems**, layer upon layer of old technology that is challenging to integrate and update. Many consultants advise on process, helping a company achieve efficiencies, for instance in their supply chain, through outsourcing and using enterprise resource planning.

The agencies, consultants and advisers summarised so far are known collectively as **professional service firms**.

We take a closer look at them as businesses in the next chapter.

CHAPTER 7

HOW PROFESSIONAL SERVICE FIRMS WORK

Partnership model – partners – lockstep – associates – trainees – fee-earners – senior associate – salaried partner – equity partners – joint and several liability – limited liability partnerships (LLPs) – time recording – Stephen Mayson – RULES – Levers of Profitability – rate – chargeable time – moral editing – utilisation – leverage – expenses – speed – work-in-progress (WIP) – lock-up – working capital requirement – David Maister – commoditisation – client relationship management (CRM) – Pareto Principle – PSF strategy – Porter's Five Forces – Henry Mintzberg

You need to know something about professional service firms (PSFs) for a number of reasons:

- You may end up working for one. That's because as more of the economy becomes service-based, so more graduate trainees are joining PSFs.
- If you don't work for one you may still end up using one. For example, you may join, say, a manufacturing company or a retail chain and, as you move into management, you may supervise your company's relationship with one or more suppliers of professional services to your organisation.

Besides, a lot of professionals who start out in PSFs go in-house. That is, they join client organisations (in the various internal functions explained earlier). In their new role they may put work out to external PSFs. You may be working alongside them so need to know how PSFs operate and charge.

In this chapter we explores PSFs as businesses in their own right.

The Partnership Model

Traditionally, PSFs were partnerships. They were owned by the senior people (called **partners**) who worked in them. The partners shared out the profits of the partnership between them. The most traditional way of doing this was called **lockstep**, meaning that your share went up year-on-year in line with your seniority in the partnership.

Below the partners were **associates** and below them were **trainees**. All of these people – partners, associates and trainees – were **fee-earners**, that is, they did work that was charged out to clients and it was this work that lay at the heart of what a PSF did. As these partnerships got bigger they introduced further categories of fee-earner such as **senior associate** (or managing associate) and **salaried partner**. Salaried partners weren't owners but having the title of partner gave them prestige and impressed clients. The real owners were called **equity partners**.

If you joined a partnership as a trainee your goal was to become a partner. But to become a partner was exceptionally difficult. For every ten associates only one might become a partner. The others would leave to try their luck elsewhere, usually at inferior firms. This was known as 'up or out'.

These partnerships were like very exclusive clubs. To become a partner you had to be technically outstanding at what you did (as a lawyer, accountant, actuary, etc). Clients tended to be institutional – that is, they were big companies and banks that had used the same firm for generations. There wasn't much competition between firms and clients very rarely switched. Partners often saw themselves as present custodians of the firm for future generations.

Because firms were owned by their equity partners they tended to be conservative and risk-averse. This was partly because historically every partner was liable for the entire partnership's liabilities, both in conjunction with other partners (jointly) but also on his or her own (severally) – known as **joint and several liability**. For this reason, banks (for example) tended to be naturally cautious. But once they incorporated (switched from being partnerships to companies) with limited liability and external shareholders, many commentators felt this natural caution went out of the window and they became much bigger risk-takers.

So far I've adopted a historic tone because the top investment banks and global accounting, law and consultancy firms are no longer small partnerships. They are now big multinational organisations with several thousand partners and are run along corporate lines. Many are now **limited liability partnerships** or **LLPs** which means they are closer to companies in structure and individual partners no longer bear joint and several liability. So they don't look much like traditional partnerships. Some have gone the whole way and become listed companies. But there are many smaller PSFs that remain much closer to traditional partnerships.

One other thing that has changed is the level of competition between them. The old institutional client relationships have broken down and clients (the word that PSFs use for customers) now regularly switch between PSFs. This has changed the role of the professional fee-earners within them. In the old days if you were really good at what you did (a great lawyer or accountant, for example) that was enough to be successful.

Now, however, partners – as owners of the business – need to spend their time doing things other than the actual work itself. Doing the work should largely be delegated down to more junior fee-earners. This frees up the partner to do these other things – such as winning new clients, winning more work from existing clients and fronting up the work to them. A big part of being a partner is about keeping clients happy and partners will expect juniors to get involved in this (which is also good training for becoming a partner).

This is a critical reason for being commercially aware. If you are a professional in a PSF you need to understand your client's business.

The Levers Of Profitability

Whether you are going to work in one or be a client of one, you need to know how PSFs make money.

Some PSFs operate in sectors where clients expect them to charge a percentage of the transaction amount (banking, property) or a percentage of the spend (advertising) or assets under management (fund managers). But many PSFs have traditionally charged by time spent on a project. Their fee-earners had hourly rates at which they were charged out to clients.

This basis of charging (called **time recording**) remained in place for decades despite at least two obvious flaws. The first is that the longer you take the more you charge. In other words, hourly rates reward the inefficient. Second, a client armed with a PSF's hourly rates still has no idea how long a job will take and therefore how much it will cost. Nevertheless this basis of charging persisted and even though clients now demand alternative fee structures (which we'll come to later), the hourly rate is still the way many PSFs account internally for their 'costs of production' (their fee-earners' time).

Stephen Mayson, a top management consultant who has worked extensively in the legal sector, devised a model called **RULES** or the **Levers of Profitability** which explains the economics of PSFs based on time charging. The rate charged was Mayson's starting point.

Rate – this is the rate per hour at which the PSF's fee-earners (those whose work is charged to clients) are billed to clients. The more senior the fee-earner, the higher the hourly rate. The point that Mayson made here was that the headline rate (the one quoted to clients) is eroded by discounts, the under-recording of time spent, and write downs (deciding not to bill all the time recorded). These can reduce the headline rate by as much as half.

The under-recording of **chargeable time** can be accidental or deliberate – accidental where a fee-earner is working across several matters or projects and time slips between the cracks; or deliberate where the partner has agreed, say, a fixed fee with the client and then encourages more junior fee-earners to 'adjust' time spent accordingly. This is called **moral editing** and is bad because it gives the PSF a distorted picture of how long it actually takes to get a particular type of work done.

In any case, much of a fee-earner's time is non-chargeable, because they are involved in business development or training juniors or administration, none of which can be charged to clients. Fee-earners can spend as much as two hours at work for every hour of chargeable time.

Aside from Rates, Mayson identified four other factors or Levers.

Utilisation – this is how busy a PSF keeps its fee-earners. They can't all be busy all the time. But if the partners fail to bring in new clients and new work, the more junior fee-earners will sit around with nothing useful to do.

Leverage – this is the ratio of partners (the owners of the business) to the other fee-earners. Mayson showed that, to make the level of profit partners expect, they have to employ and manage others to do much of the work. But he also showed that leverage only works if partners attract the sort of business that can actually be delegated downwards and be done by more junior fee-earners.

Expenses – obviously a PSF like any other business needs to keep its costs down. But Mayson's work showed that in fact their two biggest sources of expense – premises and people – are difficult to manage short-term. Offices are rented on long leases that can't be easily shortened and firing people is expensive in redundancy costs and leaves a resource gap in the firm for the future. Variable costs (which increase the busier a firm becomes) are themselves only a small part of a PSF's overall outgoings – electricity, paper and so on.

Speed – this is the speed with which a PSF converts the work it does for a client into cash at the bank. Until a PSF sends a client a bill for the work done that work is called **work-in-progress** or **WIP**. As soon as the client is sent a bill that client owes the PSF money and is therefore a debtor. Once the bill is paid the WIP has been turned into cash. The period from starting on the work to getting paid for it is called **lock-up**.

In the meantime (during the time the work is WIP) the PSF is funding outgoings such as rent and salaries. This means there is a cash flow gap. The accounting term for this is **working capital requirement**. It's the amount of cash a firm needs to cover the unbilled WIP and the unpaid debtors (the period of lock-up).

It's usually provided by a loan or capital paid in by the partners. In either case there is a cost: interest on the loan; or interest the partners would otherwise have earned on their capital. So that cost reduces the overall profitability of the work done. By reducing lock-up a firm increases profitability.

Managing The Levers

The point about Mayson's work is this. These five 'Levers' as he called them are the only ways in which a PSF's profit can be improved.

Some can be acted upon more quickly than others. You can raise your rates overnight. But will clients accept them if they are out of line with the market? You can improve lock-up by accelerating cash collection, but this is a one-off benefit. If you let WIP and debtors build up again your profitability will once again worsen.

Some are structural: leverage is a reflection of the way the PSF is staffed at all levels and is not easy to change overnight. Utilisation is about how busy your people are. It requires more work to be brought into the firm and a change in culture to motivate people to work harder. Neither can happen quickly. Expenses may seem easy to cut. But reducing the biggest costs causes structural change – in the number of people you have and the office space you use.

The Commoditisation Of Professional Services

The market-leading PSFs want to maintain high Rates. But David Maister (another management guru) explained why those Rates are continually subject to downward pressure from clients. He saw that it was because professional services are subject to continual **commoditisation**.

He saw that any area of professional service starts off as 'expert' (like rocket science or brain surgery) but rapidly becomes 'experience' work and then 'efficiency'. While professionals regard what they do as rocket science (expert), in reality little of it is. Most of it is experience work requiring no real technical brilliance or insight but simply knowledge gained from having done it before. And over time this experience work becomes efficiency, meaning that it can be done by anyone with adequate supporting processes and supervision, even by artificial intelligence.

In short, almost all professional services are subject to commoditisation through Maister's 3Es (expert, experience, efficiency) to which Mayson added a fourth – extinction. This means that if a firm's specialisms remain static the Rates it can command will get eroded over time.

Client Relationship Management

And with clients themselves much more prepared to move around, it is up to the professionals in a PSF to go out and win more business from existing clients and new clients to replace those that move elsewhere. In the past, when professional service firms had only a few dozen partners and didn't have extensive international networks, the relationship between the firm and its major clients could be conducted through one or two partners.

Now, however, professional service firms are global organisations with thousands of partners, many different areas of practice, and offices all over the world – and their clients are equally large and complex – so a more organised approach is necessary. This is done through **client relationship management** (**CRM**).

CRM makes use of databases to track and share information about the most important contacts at a client, who in the firm knows them, the degree and nature of activity between the firm and the client contacts, and the details and outcomes of marketing initiatives by the firm towards the client. Professionals in the firm will meet regularly to share information about the client and devise and pursue business development strategies.

The aim throughout is to widen and deepen relations with the client, to make the relationship stronger and more 'institutionalised' with the aim of getting better, more profitable work from a wide selection of people at the client, feeding a wider number of practice areas in the PSF.

Many professional service firms apply the Pareto Principle to their CRM activities. The **Pareto Principle** says that 80% of your business comes from 20% of your clients and it's this 20% you need to focus on. Applying the Pareto Principle encourages professional service firms to focus on a small number of core clients who produce the largest proportion of the firm's income. The firm will try to get close to those clients by fostering a web of contacts at different organisational levels, and understanding client strategies and where the buying power lies. This is all classic CRM.

Clients want professional advisers who are commercially aware – who understand and are interested in business in general and a client's commercial objectives and strategy in particular. Getting involved in these CRM activities is a good way for you to practise your own business development skills and is something all PSFs value.

Professionals Sell Themselves

One thing that hasn't changed is the importance of individual professionals in selling themselves and their firms to clients. PSFs provide advice – an intangible service – that is embodied and fronted up by the people who provide it.

So clients go to a particular firm both because of its brand but also, crucially, because people at the client like the particular fee-earners who look after their work.

When a client buys a professional service firm's services it is buying at two levels. It is buying the firm's brand (the way a consumer buys the brand of a bar of chocolate). But it is also 'buying' the firm's people in whom the client has, using Maister's words, 'faith, trust and confidence'. Because the service is provided by fee-earners, they are a crucial part of the firm's offering.

By contrast the consumer who buys the bar of chocolate never meets the people involved in its manufacture, marketing, distribution or sale – apart from the person at the checkout. This is where professional services are crucially different from, say, FMCGs.

This is why in a professional service firm it's the fee-earners – the professionals who do the work – who are also the people who need to sell it. A large part of commercial awareness is understanding this and being prepared and able to get involved.

Pure technical excellence is no longer sufficient to ensure satisfied clients. It's only part of the package that a professional service firm provides. The package also includes process, client relationship management and – yes – commercial awareness. As a work type moves from expertise to experience to efficiency these other aspects of service provision become more important.

The skills involved here are all around client service. Providing great client service isn't conceptually difficult and needs to be done at all levels. But it does require a willingness to put yourself in the client's shoes and see things from their perspective – all part of commercial awareness.

Professional Service Firms And Strategy

Many of the traditional strategy models apply equally to professional service firms.

Mayson showed how Porter's Five Forces applies to professional service firms. In particular he saw that, instead of Suppliers, professional service firms rely on a continuing pool of talent to recruit from. In terms of Entrants, there are many examples of professional service firms moving into other firms' sectors (accountancy into law, consulting into technology). Substitutes are alternatives: a client that has its own in-house lawyers instead of using external law firms; a multinational that develops its own M&A expertise in-house rather than using an external investment bank.

Henry Mintzberg, a celebrated strategy thinker, saw that professional service firms are uniquely dependent on their people to interact with clients, selling services to clients and doing the work that results from those sales. This means that professional service firms' strategies are uniquely 'bottom-up' whereas traditional corporate strategies are 'top-down' (top-down being the old style of command-and-control corporate planning). By contrast fee-earners are at the coal-face dealing daily with clients and getting a sense of what is happening in the market from that constant interaction with clients. The fee-earners can then feed this information up the organisation. Mintzberg also said that strategy can be 'emergent' – you can see an organisation's strategy evolve in the way it responds to these external market stimuli.

Mayson in his work was frustrated by the fact that the top professional service firms in the same sector often had similar strategies (for instance, aiming to advise the biggest corporates wherever they were around the world) which therefore did not act as a differentiator. Yet they were still successful. He concluded that what matters is not their espoused business strategies but what he called their **normative strategies**. Norms are values.

Mayson said that professional service firms ultimately differentiate themselves by their **culture** (remember McKinsey? 'The way we do things around here'). Clients, said Mayson, develop relationships with those firms whose norms they share (Maister's 'faith, trust and confidence') – in other words, which they like. In short it's a firm's people and their shared culture that are its USP.

The professional service firms that manage RULES, CRM and strategy the best are the ones that end up with the best work for the best clients and so attract the best people, which in turn leads to the best work for the best clients, and so on.

We're now going to look in detail at how they win and do this work – if you understand this you will impress any professional service firm where you interview for a job.

CHAPTER 8

THE 3 Ps OF PSFs

Pitching – competitive tender – long list – invitation to tender (ITT) – request for particulars (RFP) – short list – panel – pre-qualified – low-ball – trophy client – to pitch or not to pitch? – pitching as a strategic decision – identifying the client's key drivers – design the interview – the structure of the interview – features v. benefits – analyse the competition / move the goalposts – rehearse the interview – aftermath – pricing – value for money (VFM) – fixed price – alternative fee structures – project management – a simple PM methodology – scoping and pricing – contingencies – the known unknowns – project scope – scope creep – project creep – planning – monitoring progress against the plan – post-project debrief – a helpful PM tool – trade-off triangle – strategic impact

In the last chapter we started to look inside professional service firms, at the economics of how they work. We looked at the partnership model and the traditional way of charging clients by the hourly rate. We saw how sophisticated professional service firms manage their client relationships and the commoditisation of their services, and how their strategies are beginning to move from the emergent and normative (how we do things round here) to an expression of what work a firm wants to do for which types of client.

In this way professional service firms have moved away from the traditional partnership model based on institutional clients and hourly rates. Instead, driven by competitive pressures and client resistance to fees, they focus increasingly on how they get work, how they cost it and how they do it: pitching, pricing and project management – which I call the 3 Ps of professional service firms. Every firm addresses these three interlinking and overlapping activities in a slightly different way, reflecting its culture.

1. Pitching

When companies want to retain professional service firms they do it by **competitive tender**, also known as a **pitch**. The client will put together a list of possible firms to choose from. This is called a **long list**. The client will then send each firm on the long list a document setting out what the client wants. This document is called an **ITT** (**invitation to tender**) or an **RFP** (**request for particulars**). The two mean the same thing.

The invited firms – and there may be as many as a dozen on the long list – will either pitch or decide not. Each firm that decides to pitch will submit a response to the ITT or RFP setting out why it should be chosen. The client will read through these submissions and draw up a **short list** of which firms it wants to interview. The short list will typically be three or four firms long.

Each short-listed firm will be invited to an interview (either face-to-face or, increasingly in international business, by video link). On the basis of the interviews the client will select a winner.

Some bids are 'paper bids' where the client chooses on the basis of the written proposals alone.

Sometimes the client may narrow the choice down to two firms and give each a similar task to see how each firm works and then use that to decide the winner.

Typically a pitch will be for a specific project or transaction. But increasingly big companies and banks use the pitch process to assemble a **panel** of firms to provide more routine advisory services or to undertake a series of projects or transactions. The panel may be put in place for a specific period of, say, two or three years. So the rewards for the successful firms can be big. However, being appointed from the pitch simply enables each winning firm to join the panel alongside the others. Once on the panel the firms will be invited to bid alongside each other for individual pieces of work. Since all the firms on the panel are able to do the work (they are said to be **pre-qualified**), successful bids often come down to price. A firm that proves itself to be uncompetitive by being consistently outbid will in due course be ejected by the client from the panel. There are always other firms clamouring to get on a big client's panel. It will have to make way for other firms prepared to price more competitively.

Panels can place enormous competitive strains on participating firms. Superficially the rewards are attractive. But the need to price competitively to win any work at all can lead some firms to **low-ball** (put in a deliberately low price to undercut the competition) from which they may not make any profit and may indeed make a loss.

Sophisticated firms may take the strategic decision to do this. They may gamble that being known to work for a **trophy client** (one that is prestigious) can help them to impress other clients and increase their price to them. Or that developing expertise in the specific type of work on offer can confer a market-leading position that enables the firm to charge a premium to other clients for similar work.

Professional service firms train their more senior fee-earners in how to pitch. But it helps to know about the process from the outset because you may well be asked to help with pitch preparation. You may encounter pitches earlier: firms often use pitch case studies when selecting their future trainees.

To Pitch Or Not To Pitch?

The key decision is whether to accept the invitation to pitch or not. It sounds obvious, but many professional service firms are so flattered to be invited to tender that they fail to question whether to pitch at all and instead blunder on. They should at least be asking themselves the following:

- Can we expect to win this?
- Should we, at the very least, be short-listed?
- Do we have relevant expertise and track record?
- Are we prepared to invest the time to win?
- Who are our competitors likely to be?
- What are our USPs?

To pitch successfully – and there is little point in pitching unless you are going to win – requires an enormous amount of time. In professional service firms, time is money in that it is time that could be spent doing chargeable work – work for clients which can be billed.

So unless a firm is prepared to invest this time (which in a big pitch can run to hundreds of hours) don't bother. A firm needs to be convinced it has every chance of winning before deciding to tender. If it is in any doubt – usually because it lacks expertise, track record or resource – it should decline. Instead, the firm should tell the client which types of work and projects it does want to be considered for in the future. I have done this and it works, because doing so shows the client that the firm knows where its real strengths lie.

Pitching As A Strategic Decision

However, there are exceptional circumstances when a firm will pitch even though it lacks relevant experience. I mentioned earlier that firms will pitch for business that is loss-making for strategic reasons – trophy client, honing expertise – but it requires a long-term view of the investment at the expense of short-term profit. This is not easy for any business to do.

For instance, a firm may take a strategic decision to build a new area of expertise. It may spend a number of years deliberately low-balling to win the work and increase its experience and market share in this new area. It will need to be prepared to invest in such speculative pitches with little chance of immediate success, and to do so over a period. In other words, the firm needs to be committed to doing so, using profits generated in other areas of the business to support this effort.

A top consulting firm did this very successfully. It told clients upfront that it lacked the track record in the work under consideration. But it said that (1) it had identified this area of work as strategically important to it, (2) it would put its best people on the job and (3) it would charge the client half the normal rate.

This combination of honesty and commitment was persuasive. The firm was market-leading in all other areas of its business. It had a reputation for original solutions. Its consultants were amongst the smartest in the market. Who wouldn't want the best people at a top consulting firm working on their job at half price? This was a brilliant piece of strategic decision-making – as one might expect from that particular firm.

Once the firm has decided, it needs to respond to the client as quickly as possible, accepting the invitation to tender. From now the firm will be judged by the client on every interaction between them. So this is a test of the firm's speed of response.

Identifying The Client's Key Drivers

The key to winning any pitch is identifying and understanding the client's key drivers (also known as 'hot buttons') behind its decision to go out to tender.

These usually have little to do with the PSF's expertise and everything to do with the client's own situation, its own anxieties and concerns.

Professionals, in pitches, major on their own expertise and track record. But clients tend to take that as read. If you aren't up to the job it is unlikely that you would have been on the long list. What the client wants are professionals who understand what is keeping the client's people awake at night and who are able to address those issues.

There will be a number of reasons why a client has initiated a pitch. Some may be obvious concerns (such as saving money or buying in expertise the client lacks). Some may be less obvious. Some may not even be concerns that the client has articulated. These are the client's hot buttons – the issues which will determine who it appoints.

For the PSF to address these successfully requires a lot of information (research) about the client as well as deep analysis and imagination. Once it has worked out the client's hot buttons it should seek confirmation from the client that its analysis is correct, before submitting the tender.

Such a pre-pitch discussion helps the PSF work out what the client's real concerns are. It can also help the PSF to move the goal posts – often the client does not actually know what it wants until someone comes along and helps it to define its needs. The PSF which does this has an edge over the rest. Some PSFs may decide not to proceed further unless the client is prepared to make time for this pre-pitch discussion.

Design The Interview First

Professionals are very good at writing the submission because they tend to be literate and it's within their comfort zone. They may spend hours wordsmithing it.

Then as soon as they learn they're short-listed they go into a panic. Because they've now got to prepare for an interview and most professionals hate that.

So the trick is to design the submission document around the interview. Work backwards from the interview to draft the submission so that the submission document supports and follows the structure of the presentation in the interview.

The assumption is that you will be short-listed. Because if you're not going to get short-listed why are you bothering to submit at all? So work out what you are going to say in the interview before drafting the submission.

The hot buttons provide the structure for both.

One reason for adopting the same structure for both is that the people on the client's side attending the interview may not have read the submission. Often they are brought in at the last minute as the intended interviewers are called away at short notice. So do not assume that those across the table have read the submission document in great detail. They often haven't.

Some clients lay down the format of the tender document, so that all PSFs are required to follow exactly the same structure, to make comparisons between them easier. Even if you have to do this, you can subvert the process by setting out the hot buttons in a short covering letter; or attach the information the client has requested as appendices.

The Structure Of The Interview

Most clients try to see short-listed PSFs in a single day. It means they can remember them all when deciding. So each PSF is usually restricted to an hour.

Even so, it is very tiring from the client's point of view hearing the same points over again (I know because as a consultant I attended many pitches as an adviser to the client).

So the best pitches aren't all presentation. Instead they are one-third presentation and two-thirds Q&A (questions and answers), allowing the client to quiz the PSF team. The best pitches turn this into a discussion, which enables the client to see what working with the PSF would feel like.

An interview or meeting is a notoriously inefficient medium for transferring information from one person to another. This is why the hot buttons provide the structure since they address the client's real concerns (as confirmed by the pre-pitch discussion).

A simple template for such an interview is this: tell the client what the hot buttons are; get each member of the team to discuss one or more of them; open the discussion up for questions from the client (the Q&A section); recap the hot buttons; and, by then, you will have exhausted the time you have been allotted.

Features Vs. Benefits

Once you've drafted the submission, read it through. Do sentences and paragraphs start with 'we' all the time? If so, recast them to put the emphasis on 'you' (the client).

Anything you say in the submission must pass two tests.

The first is the 'so what?' test. 'We have the latest technology.' So what? To answer that, you have to explain why the latest technology should mean anything to the client, given the client's set of circumstances.

The second test (which helps answer the first) is 'which means that...' So: 'We have the latest technology, which means that we will be able to set up an extranet so that we can communicate efficiently with you.' This turns a feature of the PSF (technology) into a benefit for the client (quick and efficient reporting by the PSF). Hey presto.

Analyse The Competition / Move The Goalposts

Work out who the competitors are (try asking the client; at worst the client will say no; often the client will tell you who else is tendering). Then work out what they will claim as their USPs. Then make sure that in your submission you demonstrate that your USP is what matters.

For example, let's say that you are an engineer and the client is responsible for the construction of a toll road in a less-developed country called Ruritania. Your PSF has plenty of expertise in toll roads but has never done a project in Ruritania. Your competitor has experience of projects in Ruritania but is weak on toll roads. Your pitch – from submission to interview – must be designed to stress that what matters is knowledge of toll roads, not the particular country where the road is being built: in other words, that local conditions are secondary to toll-road know-how.

By doing this you start to outflank your competitor, because you can predict exactly what it will be majoring on (the importance of having previous knowledge of Ruritania). Doing this will move the goalposts in the client's mind: what will matter is knowledge of toll roads not previous experience of Ruritania.

Rehearse The Interview

The professional service firm must take along the team who will do the work as well as one of the firm's leaders – clients like to see the people they will be working with; and they like to feel flattered that they are important. The client will always say that it wants to see the team who will do the work – but don't make the mistake of thinking that the client doesn't want to be flattered too.

The firm should ensure that everyone in the team has something to say – even the most junior team member (who may be you).

Rehearse the FAQs – the firm needs to put a lot of thought into the questions the client's representatives are likely to ask, and how to answer them, especially on price (which we cover in detail later).

Usually a pitch team will meet three times to plan the interview. First to work out what each team member will say ('In the interview I am going to talk about..') then to start to use the language they will actually use and, by the third meeting, using the words they will actually say. Rehearsing is good. But over rehearsing can make the team jaded and a bit too polished. Passion beats polish every time.

Don't read from a script. It is boring, stilted and removes eye contact. If you must, use brief notes written on one or more cards. But, above all, remember that if you forget to say anything the client won't know because they didn't know what you were supposed to say. And if it's really important one of the others on the team will say it anyway.

Decide whether to use any audiovisuals (a slide deck for instance). I myself distrust technology. A slide deck fixes you with a given order of topic. If the discussion is wide-ranging the slides may be a hindrance. It may be better to use a printout of the slides instead. But be warned. As soon as you hand the printout over the people from the client will immediately read through it all.

One of the better 'leave behinds' I've seen (and used myself) is an A3 'place mat' with pictures and descriptions of the firm's team along the top (they need to sit in the order on the placemat) and the bulk of the space given over to a process map (in the case of the toll road project it may be a map of the world showing all of the previous toll road projects the firm has worked on). You hand over a copy to each person from the client across the table and leave plenty of space on it for them to jot notes.

Then at the end of the day once they've seen all the professional service firms that are pitching they will have a visual and memorable reminder of your firm, the team and its experience.

Aftermath

Afterwards call the client and ask whether there is anything else the interviewers need to know: if you are not the last PSF to be seen, it's possible that a competitor presenting after you has raised an issue in their minds that they haven't considered before so you need the chance to be able to cover it. Also, be prepared to have a further discussion about fees: the PSF may be asked for its 'best and final' price.

If you lose, don't back away in embarrassment. After all, the client wouldn't have short-listed your PSF if it didn't think you were any good. It knows you have invested a lot of time in the process and it's indebted to you for taking part. If you lose, ask the client why. It will be useful feedback for next time. And ask if you can stay in touch. The client will say yes: it is indebted to you and it's in the client's interest to do so.

The top consulting firm I mentioned knew it would lose a lot of pitches early on. So it always made a point of staying in regular contact with the client afterwards. What this consulting firm also knew is that the pitching medium is often inefficient and can be decided on 'chemistry' alone. The winner may have made promises it can't keep.

So the consulting firm would remain in regular contact with the client. On occasion it would even be asked to take over a project it had initially lost but which had subsequently gone off the rails. So for it, losing a pitch wasn't the end of the process of winning a client but just a temporary setback. That's because it had decided early on that this was a client it really wanted. Why else bother to pitch?

One of the major points the client will want to discuss in the pitch is price.

2. Pricing

We saw previously that firms historically used business models based on charging clients for the time taken on a piece of work (Rate, the first of Stephen Mayson's five Levers). But clients see that charging by time rewards the less efficient and provides little certainty as to the overall outcome because they don't know how long the firm is going to take.

Instead they want the fees fixed upfront. And they want to know what they are paying for, not in terms of the firm's input (its experience and expertise) but in terms of the output (how whatever the firm does benefits the client). In particular they will want to know the **VFM (value for money)** that the work provides. In other words the client (a business itself) will be saying: 'How does the work you do further my commercial objectives and how can I put a price on the value of your work?'

Traditionally, professionals are poor at explaining this to clients. But clients will think it odd and unbusinesslike if a professional service firm which professes to be a business adviser (and a successful business in its own right) is unable to discuss money.

Price is a complex issue, not least because after a job has been done, a complaint about price is often a complaint about other things involving service.

From the outset I think clients have six things going through their minds – consciously or unconsciously – when they ask about price, though not all at the same time or with the same emphasis.

a. **How much will this cost?** When buying anything, consumers want to know what the cost will be. Buying professional services is no different. Clients always have budgets they work to. Like anybody else they want to know how much something will cost before they commit to buying it (not least because with professional services it is so much harder switching advisers mid-stream; you can't just put it back in the box and return it to the shop).

Ideally, professional service firms should be able to quote clients fixed prices for particular jobs. Some can and do. Estates agents do. So do investment banks. They work on a 'swings-and-roundabouts' business model. Some deals never happen so they can't charge anything. So for those deals that do they need a large margin to cover those that don't.

For many professional service firms that traditionally charged by time this has been a major shock. Where a firm charges by time and quotes various hourly rates, the client will press for a **fixed price** (or at the very least an estimate or a quote). A fixed price puts any risk of a cost overrun on the PSF since a fixed price is what the client will pay regardless of how the job turns out.

b. **What's the market rate?** This is a price-check. It's the client saying: if I were to shop around, would the rates you are quoting me reflect the rates of other comparable PSFs (smaller, less specialist ones may quote less; larger professional service firms with greater market presence, reputation and brand may quote more).

Of course, one problem with hourly rates is that they only tell one side of the story. They fail to tell clients how long a job will take. In a sense, the less efficient a firm, the longer the job will take and the higher the bill. So hourly rates are open-ended and reward inefficiency. Which, again, is a reason for quoting a price-per-job and not just a rate.

c. **What's this worth to me?** Whereas the previous question is an objective test this is subjective. The same job may be worth completely different amounts depending on a client's own aims, goals and situation. For one client the project may be routine. For another it may be the key to a whole new strategy. Those professionals that know their clients well will have a good sense of this – and flex what they charge accordingly. For example, if getting the job done to a tight deadline is 'mission critical' to the client, ask for a success fee or premium for doing so.

d. **How many of these have you done before?** Here, price is a proxy for experience. The more of this type of work you have done the more precise your ability to price it. If you tell me you've done plenty of these before but can't then give me a quote or fixed fee, I may begin to wonder whether you've done quite as many as you are making out. The greater the track record, the more accurate and precise the figure should be, contingencies notwithstanding. Price as a proxy for track record is far more important to clients than professional service firms realise.

e. **How much of your inefficiency am I paying for?** Sophisticated clients are beginning to understand how inefficient and inconsistent professional service firms can be in service delivery. They know that some types of professional are only now adapting to large deals where they have to project manage big teams between time zones. As a result some work can be duplicated, other work wasted and team members have to be brought up to speed to cover for absences (for instance for vacations and sickness). They also know that juniors learn on-the-job and not all of their time is productive. Cute clients (the street-smart) will negotiate hard on the make-up of the firm's team and require any changes to be agreed with them in advance, with the professional service firm absorbing any resultant costs.

f. If I pay you more, will you go the extra mile? This is the upside of the previous one. However hard clients can be with their advisers they do genuinely appreciate them. This is saying: 'I really want you and your PSF on this job because I know and trust you and am prepared to pay more for that. And if I have excessive demands that you meet (and I wouldn't be using you if you couldn't) I understand that I need to pay for that too, for going above and beyond the normal call of duty.'

Professionals underestimate this factor – but the key is to negotiate it into the price at the outset, not wait in the hope of a reward at the end – which reminds me: there is a psychology about when to bill. Bill immediately after the project is complete – as soon as you can, while the client is feeling euphoric that (1) it's over and (2) they won't be seeing as much of you as they have done but (3) before the client forgets what a big deal it was. By the way, clients forget astonishingly quickly and often need reminding. Billing promptly to convert work-in-progress into debtors and then collecting the amount billed quickly to reduce lock-up is also good for cash flow – sound familiar?

Alternative Fee Structures

Smart professionals have an array of pricing structures at their disposal, designed to allocate risk more fairly between them and the client. Here are some pricing alternatives, known as **alternative fee structures**.

Structure *Explanation*	*Comment*
Hourly rate *Rate per seniority of professional*	Open ended Places risk on the client Meaningless in terms of likely overall bill Difficult for client to police
Estimate *Best guess at overall cost*	Not binding on professional service firm – but a reputational commitment
Quote *Best guess but more binding*	Client may view this as a fixed price but professional service firm may see it as merely an intention

Fixed price *The price, fixed at the outset, that the firm will bill*	Certain outcome – but will the firm build in too large a cushion to offset lack of project management skills? Or will the work end up being unprofitable for the firm?
Ceiling *Upper limit*	Maximum fee fixed at the outset but with no agreed minimum so puts the risk on the PSF; often confused with fixed price
Fixed price + Override *Provides scope for change order – this works by fee being fixed at, say, 250k with PSF taking any hit above 250k until, say, 270k is reached, then client is back on the clock*	Suggests firm has thought it through and has track record But, once 250k is reached, the firm may race to ensure 270k is reached quickly; and thereafter entirely at client's risk
Discount *Reduction in hourly rate or overall bill to reflect volume of work*	Often too easily offered by firms without fully understanding the impact on profitability (on average a discount of 10% can reduce profit by a third)
Blended hourly rates *Rates of all professionals on the team are blended to result in a single hourly rate for all professionals involved*	Encourages delegation, with the risk of partners being less involved than they should be Needs policing of team members No way for client to check that the overall time spent is appropriate
Partner-based rates *All work is charged out at the firm's highest hourly rates*	This means that junior time is effectively not charged unless the firm thinks it has been particularly valuable. Disincentive for delegation – so guarantees partner involvement from the client's perspective, but often makes it more expensive than is necessary

Value billing *Client pays PSF what client feels work is worth – after the event*	Good in principle but firms are scared to offer this – it requires the firm to trust the client and the client to have a full understanding of the work involved But it is ideal if it works because it encourages efficiency and communication by the firm and deepens the client relationship
Incentive billing *Additional payment for achieving results*	Risk may be shifted too far on to the firm if some outcomes are outside its control
Task-based billing *Specific elements of a project are fixed-price*	Excellent way of discovering a firm's true knowledge of the work – encourages a dialogue at which specifics of the deal can be carved-out or made subject to caveats Provides certainty Requires the firm to be able to 'chunk' types of project
Conditional fee *Success fee as a percentage uplift on the hourly-based fee*	The firm is only paid if the project is successful – in which case the firm gets a mark-up on what it would have charged on an hourly-rate basis – but this may not reflect a true share of what the client gains
Contingency fee *As above but firm gets a percentage of what client makes on the project*	The firm is only paid if the project is successful – but here the firm shares in the client's project proceeds
Abort fees *Fixed fee or 'no fee' arrangement with PSF if project does not complete*	Places risk on the firm But can be part of a long-term client relationship where the firm receives all of a client's work, so it can charge a premium for successful projects to offset unbilled time on aborts

These are just examples of the alternative fee arrangements that firms can discuss with clients. They enable a richer, fuller discussion to take place with the client and provide the client with a measure of control over what the firm is proposing to do. One of the biggest complaints that clients make about professional service firms and the way they work is the lack of control or input that the client feels it has over what the professional service firm is doing and how much it is charging.

I came across a professional who made a point, every week, of telling his client how much in costs had been charged up over the previous seven days. When I asked why, he said: 'It provokes a conversation. If the client thinks costs are running too high, they have a chance to say so. It means I can explain the value of what we have done when it is still uppermost in the client's mind. It also means that if there is scope creep I can raise it with the client at the earliest possibility and get their agreement to the additional work and its likely cost.'

A soon as he mentioned 'scope creep' I knew I was talking to someone who practised project management – which is the last of the three Ps.

3. Project Management

Project management (**PM**) is about how you do the work once you have got it. But undoubtedly it will be something the client wants you to talk about during the pitch.

Having a clear and tested PM can be a pitch-winner. It is also a way of capturing data from previous similar projects which can then be used to refine your pricing and process for the next one, and increase your prospects of winning it.

Any piece of work for a client should be properly project managed, especially if it involves teams of fee-earners working in different offices.

At its most basic, PM splits a job into its constituent parts, identifies the dependencies (which bits depend on others being done first), allocates the resources (fee-earners) between stages, and provides a way of monitoring progress by tracking milestones against costs.

Some professional service firms use PM techniques in their work as a matter of course – engineers and technology consultants, for example. Some consultants are PM specialists and are brought in by clients to apply PM techniques to the work undertaken by other professional service firms. PM is a professional discipline in its own right. Prince 2 is one of the most well-known methodologies, adopted and promoted by the UK government.

You might think that using PM is pretty obvious. But many professionals dislike PM. They see it as unnecessary process that cramps their professional style. Professionals enjoy the autonomy their role provides – the freedom to undertake a particular piece of work in the way they consider best. They see PM as an unnecessary constraint.

This doesn't mean that professionals don't plan. But they often carry the plan in their head (a mental back-of-an-envelope) and see their ability to do so as a hallmark of their experience. If I know how to do something why do I need the bureaucratic overlay of a PM process to spell out the obvious?

They also tend to think of PM in systems terms, as software that generates spreadsheets and Gantt charts. But PM does not have to be like this. A simple project plan is a good way of showing a client that you know what you are doing (and have done it before). It instils confidence. It also keeps the pricing on track.

Clients expect explicit, tangible PM and, indeed, think they are already paying for it. Many clients themselves use PM. So should their advisers.

A Simple PM Methodology

For any professional in a firm that doesn't have its own PM methodology, the following is a simple but proven model. There are four stages. All four stages need to be considered at the outset of the project and then they need to be reviewed at the end as part of the fourth and final stage, the debrief.

1. Scoping (And Pricing)

Scoping a job sounds obvious. But few professionals do it properly.

Imagine the scene. A client calls a partner at a professional service firm with an exciting new project for the firm to do. The partner is thrilled to receive the call since she is expected by her firm to bring in new work from clients. The last thing she wants to do is put this new job at risk. But she knows that good PM requires her to find out a bit more.

'Could I just ask you some questions about the project?' she says.

The client refuses. He is busy and doesn't have time. He says something like, 'It's the same as last time,' or 'It's just a standard project of the type I know you people are good at,' or – even worse – 'If you don't think you're up to it I'll take it elsewhere.'

So the partner is tempted to say: 'That's fine. I'll get on and do it.'

In short, the tendency when a client calls with a new piece of work is to be so pleased (and eager to please) that the partner doesn't want to do anything to jeopardise the award of the work. Professionals just want to get on with the job – much easier than engaging the client in a discussion about it.

This is a big mistake.

This initial discussion is critical. It will determine the parameters of the job and whether or not the job is brought to a successful conclusion in the client's eyes, on time and to a budget the client is happy with.

This is because you need to establish the client's critical success factors (CSFs) – what matters to the client and what will make him or her feel it's been done successfully. You need to establish a timeline. And you need to agree a price. In discussing the price you will naturally talk about contingencies.

Now it may be that the latest project is part of a pipeline of similar projects so this initial discussion isn't really needed. Fine. Keep it short. But don't abandon it. At the very least, ask the client what changes he would like to see (if any) from last time. One of clients' biggest complaints is the lack of communication and consultation on the part of PSFs they use. Even if the client says: 'No changes needed from last time', they should at least be pleased to have been asked.

Contingencies – The Known Unknowns

Contingencies are things that can go wrong. 'Something always goes wrong and we never know in advance what it is' is a common refrain among fee-earners at PSFs.

These contingencies are also called 'known unknowns'. They are known, in that they have been encountered before. But they are unknown in that for any given project the fee-earner has no idea at the outset which of these contingencies is likely to occur.

In any typical project there are between three and five major things that can go wrong. In most projects only one or two of these five contingencies happen. But you never know which ones or their impact until they occur.

This is where having a PM methodology can save the day. Part of the process (as we shall see) is to review and capture data from each project including, crucially, the known unknowns that were encountered and the impact they had on the project timeline and costs. This is then built into future pitches and projects.

If you have this data to hand when you pitch you can have a useful discussion with the client about the known unknowns. You will know the range of things that can go wrong and the likelihood of each doing so. You can price and plan accordingly.

It makes for a much richer discussion with the client about price. A PSF that knows that, for a given type of work, five possible things can go wrong and usually only one or two do, will be able to explain all of this to the client.

This will impress the client and demonstrate that the PSF knows what it's talking about and has a depth of past experience of these projects to draw on (an example of using pricing as a way of demonstrating your track record). The PSF will be able to offer the client a basic price and then an add-on for each contingency should it materialise.

This is far more persuasive than a PSF that offers a blanket price with more of a cushion built-in but for no explicit reason or, even worse, one that low-balls just to get the work at any cost.

Compare these two approaches:

Professional service firm (without the data) 'Based on our previous extensive experience we believe this work will cost £250,000 but we've allowed an uplift of £50,000 for contingencies. So we'll cap it at £300,000.'

Three quarters of the way through it's clear the job will cost £350,000. The PSF hesitates to tell the client. When it does so the client is angry. If the client insists on the cap, the PSF will have people working on the project for which it won't get paid. So the client fears the PSF may not do the best job possible. This can lead to distrust. But if the client pays in full, its own budget will be wrecked.

Professional service firm (with the data) 'We have analysed our five previous prices for similar work done for other clients. The range was £300,000 to £375,000. The reason for this is that in all of the jobs a contingency arose. We now know it is likely to be one of five possible things. Usually one, and occasionally two, might occur – hence the upper figure. We will cap it at £375,000 but as soon as we think a contingency may arise we will raise it with you to see if we can reduce its impact upfront and to give you some input into how we tackle it and what the cost outcome is likely to be. We think on this conservative basis that the cap is unlikely to be reached.'

Which is the more impressive? The second: because the PSF really sounds as if it knows what it's doing and as if it's done this before – even though the cap is higher. Its approach will give the client more confidence.

This is particularly so because clients that go to the trouble of using a pitch to award work regard that work as important and rarely regard price as the overriding selection criterion. They want to feel confident the job will be done properly. They are prepared to give the job to a higher bidder to get this reassurance.

Some clients – a minority – will take the lowest bid, come what may. But these aren't generally clients you want for the long term because they will always argue over the bill in order to pay as little as possible and generally be unappreciative of the PSF's efforts.

The only reason to want these clients is because they are big names in the market (trophy clients). In which case the PSF is pitching for prestige rather than profit, which is fine provided the PSF understands that this is what it's doing (remember the management consultancy that would do this for strategic reasons?).

From this initial discussion the partner will draw up a **project scope** with a pricing structure and get the client to agree them. This is to prevent **scope creep** (also known as **project creep**). Scope creep occurs when additional work is added to the project as it goes along (often for perfectly innocent reasons, to tackle contingencies). Unless an initial scope is in place that defines what the PSF is and isn't going to do, it is very hard to get the client to agree mid-project to any adjustment in price or timeline to cover these add-ons.

2. Planning

Then drawing up a project plan and discussing it with the client will ensure there are no surprises. It also establishes on-going dialogue with the client as a normal part of the process. At its most basic a project plan includes:

- A breakdown of a piece of work into stages
- A resource allocation (who will do what, when and how long it should take)
- Timescales
- Priorities and dependencies (what needs to be done before what)
- Costs (per stage)
- Contingencies (what may go wrong and how to tackle it)
- Cushion (allowance in time and costs for contingencies)

None of this needs a spreadsheet.

This plan becomes the spine of the project. It is used by the firm's team to work with each other and as a basis for communicating progress and issues to the client. The sort of questions the firm needs to address when drawing up the plan include:

- How will our team be organised?
- Who will be the project manager?
- How will the work be allocated?
- How will our team communicate internally and with the client?
- What will the plan look like?
- How will it be distributed and updated?
- How will changes in scope be detected?
- What will we do about them?

3. Monitoring Progress Against The Plan

Once the project is underway, progress needs to be monitored against the plan. Whenever something unexpected arises (a contingency) this needs to be raised immediately with the client. It's a mistake to start work on addressing it until the client has agreed an adjustment to the price and the timeline, and this change has been incorporated into the plan.

The sorts of issues that need to be considered when monitoring progress and reporting to the client include:

- Reporting frequency
- Client's preferred format
- Progress expressed in terms of the client's critical success factors
- Percentage of work done so far
- Any slippage against deadline
- Causes of delays / additional work
- Whether these are covered by assumptions set out in the scope of work
- Impact of delays / additional work
- Time needed to completion

It's a good idea to set up a log in which to note changes of scope and unexpected contingencies. This will feed into the debrief and into the firm's knowledge database for future similar projects. The log should cover:

- How contingencies / overruns have been managed
- The reasons why they were unexpected
- The impact they have had on timeline and costs
- How they have been communicated to the client
- The outcomes and the reasons for them

4. Post-Project Debrief

Once the project has been completed, there should be a post-completion review. This should start with an internal team debrief involving all of the PSF's fee-earners who were involved, followed by a debrief with the client at which the final bill can be discussed and agreed.

The internal debrief should address:

- What went right
- What went wrong
- The reasons why in either case
- The impact on time and costs
- The lessons to learn for the future
- The extent to which the client's critical success factors have been met
- How this can be demonstrated to the client
- Where and how the firm provided value for money

In doing this the firm's team will be reminding itself (as it has been throughout) of:

- The client's critical success factors
- The initial fee quote v. what's on the clock

- The assumptions set out in the project scope
- The timetable / deadline
- Contingencies that arose and how they were addressed
- The reasons for any overruns
- The importance and strength of the client relationship and the likelihood of future work

It's easy to lose sight of these things once the project is over and a fresh job is underway. Reiterating them at the internal debrief will remind the firm's team of its project achievements and enable it to demonstrate with confidence to the client how the client's critical success factors have been met.

Clients generally welcome project debriefs. At the very least they allow a client to raise any issues it hasn't had the opportunity to voice so far while reminding the client of what the firm has done and why, the achievement of the client's critical success factors and, ultimately, the value for money of the firm's work.

Then – and this is the real strength of this process – the project (and in particular the information from the debriefs) needs to be filed in the firm's knowledge systems alongside details of similar projects. Recording these outcomes and debriefs and adding them to the firm's knowledge database can transform a firm's win rate at pitches and improve its dialogue with clients.

Professional service firms that do this build up an invaluable database of similar projects – how much each cost, whether it was finished on time and to budget, the contingencies encountered and how they were resolved, any scope creep, the fees paid, any write-downs (reductions offered in the final bill) and the reasons why. This level of insight will inform the next pitch and make the interview with the prospective client a much richer and rewarding opportunity, increasing markedly the firm's chances of winning it.

Now that you are familiar with the stages of project management you can see why all of this needs to be considered not just at the end of the project but also at the outset. Being this well prepared will make the project run more smoothly.

A Helpful PM Tool

There is a classic bit of project management theory that helps resolve a common issue in projects: how can you achieve the best quality outcome to time and within budget? In an ideal world, time and budget would be unconstrained and the quality of the project would not be compromised.

This is where the project management **trade-off triangle** comes in. The three corners of the triangle are Time, Cost and Quality. Improve Quality and the job may take longer (Time) and/or be more expensive (Cost). Shrink the deadline

(Time) and Quality will suffer or – to avoid that happening – Cost will have to increase as greater resource is committed to the project.

People in professional service firms often believe that this doesn't apply to them. They feel they can never compromise on Quality because that means stinting on their professional expertise and could be negligent. But here Quality doesn't mean technical skill. It means quality of service. You can compromise on Quality – with the client's approval. For instance, you can give an oral piece of advice that you don't back up with a written opinion. It saves time by providing a different level of service (Quality). This helps professionals see Quality from the client's point of view, not theirs.

This trade-off triangle can be a useful tool in discussing projects at the outset with clients.

The Strategic Impact

As you can begin to see, a database of similar project plans with a record of outcomes and post-completion reviews (internally and with the client) can be an incredibly useful strategic tool for a professional service firm. The firm can begin to see where it makes money, where it loses it, where projects run into trouble and how best to manage those contingencies.

This know-how can be used by the professional service firm to price similar projects more precisely, knowing how much of a cushion needs to be built in for contingencies. Using the data, it can demonstrate to clients where the contingencies lie and explain in detail how the work will be managed, which increases the firm's credibility. Being able to price with precision means that quotes are more competitive.

All of this will help the firm win more pitches. This in turn will increase the firm's market share in that type of work. The more work it wins, the more it increases its expertise which in turn leads to more work. This work then becomes part of the professional service firm's core business and will be a major factor in attracting clients and talented new recruits who want to work for it.

The professional service firm can then use this core, profitable work to subsidise new areas of work (gained through low-balling) as it builds up similar databases around projects in those new fields, over time becoming more competitive.

Highly profitable types of work can also be used to support new areas or less profitable work types that need to be done to keep clients happy.

Like any business that uses the Boston Consulting Group matrix to assess its different product lines, sophisticated professional service firms 'portfolio manage' their work types – firm-wide and department-wide – to develop a spread of work, and they 'portfolio manage' their client base (think Pareto Principle).

They quantify each client's lifetime value (heard that before?) not just in terms of profit but in terms of the professional service firm's overall strategic goals. Acting for a certain client is worth a profitability trade-off if it brings other quantifiable benefits of strategic value, such as:

- Trophy – it's good to be seen to be acting for this client in the market
- Honing of expertise – this client's work keeps us at the cutting edge
- Using the whole firm – this client enables us to work across departments
- Ambassadorial – this client tells everyone else how great we are
- Training – this client provides great work to train our juniors
- Enjoyment – this clients is always great fun to work with

Sophisticated professional service firms calculate which work types they have to do (at a loss) to retain their (strategically valuable) clients (and if a client isn't strategically valuable, why have it?), and which they can do at a super-profit because they are a market leader in certain clients' eyes for that type of work.

This is how pitching, pricing and project management when taken together can transform a professional service firm's strategy.

So, now you know about corporate businesses and professional service firms. You know about the importance of customers and clients. You know what business development is and why it matters. You understand strategy and the role of money. You know how businesses are organised.

Now it's time to look at how you get a job in one.

CHAPTER 9

HOW TO GET YOUR FIRST JOB

You only need one job – how does an organisation feel to you? – Stephen Mayson's normative strategy – interviews – useless questions to ask – better questions to ask – internal facing roles – how we do things around here – culture

Now we have a full understanding of business in all its forms – companies and professional service firms (which tend to be LLPs) – let's turn to how you get a job at one of them.

There are many, many books on this topic, from how to select a career to perfecting your CV and handling the job interview. And there are many careers offices at universities and nationally that can help.

So I'm not going to regurgitate all the good advice they contain.

Rather, I'm going to look at commercial awareness in the context of getting a job and, mainly, at how you demonstrate it at interview.

You Only Need One Job

A student approached me after one of the talks I give up and down the country to say that she had sent out fifty applications and not had a single interview.

It was obvious what the issue was. If you send out that many applications, none of them will be personalised to the specific organisation. If you send out that many applications they will be generic. More importantly, if you send out that many applications you don't really know what you want to do or where you want to do it.

The point is: you only need one job. But if you don't know what it is, why should anyone who might have a job offer it to you?

You need to do a lot of research and talking to people in order to identify the organisations where you may want to work. You need to find out everything you can about an organisation before you apply to it. If you do that and really want to work there, this will come through in your application. Your application will be personal to that organisation. The more personal it is, about why you want to work there in particular, the more likely it is to catch their eye and encourage them to want to interview you.

When an organisation recruits an individual, especially a graduate first-jobber, it (the organisation) is taking on huge risk. Recruiting and training a graduate is very expensive in terms of time and money. You won't be economically productive for as much as two years while you are being trained. By my estimate it costs a law firm a quarter-of-a-million pounds to recruit and train a trainee lawyer, including all of the course fees and grants the firm pays before the person has even joined it. That is a big investment.

So the people across the table from you want to be as sure as they can be that you will be a good fit. That you will do well, will like them and will stay.

But how do they (and you) know?

I meet many students who are very successful in their academic studies. Because they have done and are doing well, they want to make sure they don't mess up when it comes to getting their first job. So they bring the same intellectual process to bear. They compare possible jobs by scoring each one against a set of factors relevant to them. In other words they turn it into an intellectual task.

In my experience this doesn't work. I think you have to go on 'feel'. The job that is right for you is the one that feels right, from the moment you walk through the organisation's doors to the people you meet at interview and beyond. The reason I say this is because if you are in an organisation where you feel happy you will do well. And if you do well your career will flourish.

These days it is much easier to move around jobs, especially when you are young, than it was when I was your age. So you can start off at a relatively small employer where, because you are happy you do really well, and then you can move to a bigger one if you want to.

But – and here's the thing – if you find an employer where you are really happy, the chances are you won't want to leave. Why would you if they give you everything – by way of training, opportunity and pay – that you want?

So how does this 'feel' thing work?

How Does An Organisation Feel To You?

This is where Stephen Mayson's normative strategy (mentioned earlier) comes in.

Mayson shows that the only real way you can tell between organisations that do similar things for similar clients is by their culture ('the way we do things round here' as McKinsey defined it).

An interview is a two-way street. You are interviewing them to be sure you want to work there. And they are interviewing you to be sure you are good enough. What if you really like the organisation and the people and you really want the job? What then?

So what the people across the table want to be sure about is that you will be a good fit in terms of their culture. The sorts of questions that they will be asking themselves about you are:

- Will you enjoy working here?
- Will you be a good learner?
- Will you work well for and with others?
- Will you stay here once we have trained you?
- Will you be flexible and responsive?
- Are you someone who will be able to deal with clients?

In order to show these people what you are like – and to demonstrate your commercial awareness – you need to imagine that you are already working there. In other words your questions should be about what will be expected of you in the role.

You'll remember that previously I talked about the pitching interview process. It's a good tip to do the same there, treating the interview as if it's the first-meeting-after-being-appointed – as long as it's not in a smug way that suggests you've got the job.

What Commercial Awareness In An Interview Is About

I understand that a lot of questions in interviews are about what is happening out there in the real world and that this passes for commercial awareness. In other words have you read about recent developments in the world (political or business) and what do you think about them?

While I think this may be useful (all employers want their people to be outward looking) I don't think this is genuine commercial awareness. It's just about knowing the news (I'm not knocking that; I just don't think it goes far enough).

Real commercial awareness is about understanding your (commercial) client. And in this context you client is your future employer: the people across the table from you.

So when it is your turn to ask questions of them I think you need to ask questions that do two things: (1) help you work out whether this really is the organisation where you want to work; and (2) show them that you really want to work here.

The sorts of questions that I understand people in your position may be encouraged to ask at interview include:

- 'How good is the training I can expect to receive?'
- 'What is your strategy – and how can I deliver it?'
- 'How soon will I be given responsibility?'
- 'How quickly will I get into management?'

These are supposed to show that you are ambitious and dynamic.

I think these are all useless. Here's why.

Why These Are Useless Questions

'How good is the training I can expect to receive?' This is useless because any large, market-leading organisation will provide you with excellent training. Why would it not? It wants you to be as economically productive as soon as possible. Small organisations, too, can provide excellent personalised training. They recruit fewer people so can spend more time on each.

'What is your strategy – and how can I deliver it?' The answer is: look on the organisation's website. That will give some indication of its strategy. But in terms of delivering it, you can't. You will be too new and too junior. There is nothing you will be able to do to help deliver it. Your job is to do your job to the best of your ability with all of the excellent training you will get. (And while we're on the subject of training don't ever say 'I can do this if you train me': most jobs worth doing have new challenges every day for which you won't have been trained. If all you needed to do a job was training then organisations wouldn't need humans.) Even the CEO has trouble delivering the organisation's strategy. So you have no chance.

'How soon will I be given responsibility?' The answer is obvious. As soon as possible and probably before you're ready for it. Responsibility is stressful. It is often about doing things just beyond your current skillset (see earlier point about training). The short answer is you will get too much responsibility way before you feel able to handle it comfortably.

'How quickly will I get into management?' This is a rubbish question too, because most first-jobbers have no idea what management is. They think it's about telling people to do things. It isn't. Even if it were, people don't as a rule do what you tell them to do if all you do is tell them to do it. At the very least they need to know why. And they generally have useful things to say about the 'how' – how it should be done.

Management in my experience is about two things.

The first is dealing with difficult people. Once you are put in charge of other people you will find that most are fine, amenable, talented, conscientious and hard-working. But one or two won't be. For whatever reason they are trouble. You have two choices. Help improve them or manage them out. Neither is easy. Both take time. In the worst cases you'll have to do both: help them improve and, when they don't, get rid of them.

But difficult people don't just exist below you in the organisation. They exist on all sides and above. They exist on all sides because all the other team leaders will be trying to get your team to accept responsibility for, and to do, things their teams should be doing. And the people above you will be difficult because they want your team to do things for which it hasn't been adequately resourced.

So that's the first fun bit about management.

The second is that your real job as a team leader is to help your team work out what it should be doing to further the organisation's objectives and then to remove all the obstacles the rest of the organisation puts in your way that prevent your team from doing it.

In other words, management (like responsibility) is not fun and you will get it way before you feel ready. Anyone who is any good quickly gets management thrust upon them.

So if these are lousy questions to ask, what are the good ones?

Better Questions To Ask

I go back to what I said earlier. You are trying to convince the people across the table that you are not a big-risk hire. Put yourself in their shoes. What will they expect of you and how well will you be able to fulfil it? To do this you need to ask questions as if you are already working there or, at least, are imagining that you are.

- 'What will I be expected to do on day one?'
- 'Who will my first boss be and how can I help them in their role?'
- 'What were the challenges you faced when starting out?'
- 'How will I know that I am on track?'

This last one is tricky. First-jobbers these days are constantly asking for feedback. But what they mean is: 'Tell me how great I am.'

What they should be asking is: 'How can I improve?' The latter is obviously inviting some sort of criticism. And this is the point about feedback. Unless it is showing you what you can do better it isn't useful at all. But people don't like giving feedback because most people are poor at receiving it. So you need to learn how to take it in the right way. Not personally and badly-meant. But as helpful guidance you are grateful to receive.

Questions That Demonstrate Commercial Awareness

None of these questions are about commercial awareness. But they are better than the ones you might otherwise ask.

No, to my mind, the questions that demonstrate your commercial awareness and understanding of the organisation to those across the table are these:

- 'How do you go about getting new business? Do you pitch for it? What techniques have worked best for you?'
- 'How do you price your work?'
- 'How do you project manage it?'
- 'What are the levers of profitability that work best in your organisation?'

(Sound familiar?)

To which the response is:

'Wow. Here's someone who really gets it. Here is someone who thinks like us.'

Because these are questions that people in organisations are asking themselves all the time.

Even, 'How do you go about CRM? What role can more junior people play?'

In other words you are putting yourself in their shoes. You are trying to see and understand their business through their eyes.

And that is what every client wants their advisers to do.

What you want the people across the table to feel as a result of the conversation they have with you is:

- 'This person wants to help'
- 'This person has thought about what we need'
- 'This person wants to be the best they can'
- 'This person sounds flexible and responsive'
- 'This person seems interested'
- 'This person could be a good fit'

What If The Role Is Internally Facing?

Now, it may be that the role you are interviewing for is internal. It doesn't have direct contact with the organisation's customers or clients and isn't to do with dealing with them directly.

But everyone in an organisation has clients. They may not be customers of the organisation but they are people in the organisation who are your customers.

Remember the man who was sweeping the floors at NASA, the US space agency, who said he was helping to put a man on the moon? He was. He wasn't building the rocket. But he was keeping the place tidy for those who were. His sense of his role gave it significance and meaning.

The scientists and engineers building the rocket knew who their clients were: the astronauts going into space who were entrusting their lives to the work the scientists and engineers were doing. And his internal clients were the scientists and engineers themselves.

When you are building a space rocket you need to work in a very clean environment. It matters how clean the floors are. A clean environment sets the tone for what you as a scientist are doing.

So whatever your role you need to have a sense of your immediate clients and your role in the organisation's mission to serve its external customers.

The man sweeping the floors had a very real sense of both. But I bet you when he got the job he didn't ask how he could help deliver NASA's strategy.

How We Do Things Around Here

There is another reason for asking the sorts of questions I've suggested.

These go to the heart of how the organisation wins, prices and does its work. These are the questions that the people across the table grapple with in their everyday lives. Your questions will impress them that you have really thought about what it is like to work there.

But – as importantly – their answers will give you a terrific sense of what it is really like to work there. In other words, their answers will tell you how they do things around here – in short, what their culture is, and whether this is a place where you want to work. And that is probably the single most important factor in deciding whether a particular organisation is for you.

Asking someone about the culture of their organisation might seem like a good question. But it is incredibly difficult to answer. Culture is all around you. It is hard to capture and put into words especially if you are within it. So asking about an organisation's culture is, in my book, another useless question and will not get you the useful answers you want.

Instead, ask these other questions about how the organisation goes about its business. In the way they are answered and in what is said you will learn what an organisation's culture is – how it feels to work here.

Right, so you've done all of that – and you've got the job at a place where you want to work! Great!

Now it's time to meet your first client.

CHAPTER 10

MEET YOUR FIRST CLIENT

Line manager – supervisor – delegation – feedback – models for feedback – BOOST – NITA feedback – appraisal – time management – working with others – working in teams

Your first client won't be a client or customer of the organisation where you're working.

Your first client will be your first boss (**line manager** or **supervisor** in business speak).

As a new recruit, you may not be unleashed on real clients just yet. But all of the skills you need can be developed by treating your supervisor – your first boss – as your first client.

Everything I've said so far about dealing with clients applies to your boss. You want to build a relationship with them to ensure that you deliver what they want.

Some of the questions you would ask a client you won't need to ask your boss because (1) you know something about their business (since you are starting to work in it yourself) and (2) you know their function in it.

When you are junior in an organisation you will receive work from your boss and other senior people through **delegation**.

Getting Work

Ideally, delegation will follow a series of steps. These include the following:

- The supervisor should select an appropriate task for the right developmental reasons (not just to shift something off their desk but because it will help in the development of, say, a new team member).
- The supervisor should also select the new team member as an appropriate delegatee for good developmental reasons rather than because they happen to be available.
- The supervisor should then prepare the briefing. In the briefing itself, the supervisor should identify the nature of the task and the client, then check the delegatee's experience and availability.
- The supervisor should specify the output they want: note, draft letter, report. Is it for their own use or to go to the client? If the client, what will the client be using it for?
- The supervisor should also specify any constraints (such as how much time to spend on it) and the deadline.
- The supervisor should then check the delegatee's understanding by getting the delegatee to reiterate what they've been told and specify what their proposed first few steps in undertaking the task will be.
- The supervisor should also set up an interim monitoring procedure, by specifying a midpoint when the delegatee can come back and report on progress.
- The supervisor should also liaise with others – the client so that the client knows who is doing the work; others in the team so they know the delegatee is busy and not to be overloaded.

- Then, once the delegatee has done the job, the supervisor should provide feedback and, finally, find further opportunities to reinforce the delegatee's development by giving them related tasks.

Typical Delegation

This is fine in theory. In practice it doesn't happen. Supervisors don't have time. More typically, delegation occurs like this:

'Here's the file. Read yourself into it. We need to respond to the client's most recent query which is on the top. Put something together for me to look at. If you have any problems, come back to me.'

Think back to what I said about project management. The issue you face as the delegatee is the same issue the professional faces at the start of a project in trying to engage the client in a discussion about the project. The client doesn't have time and is generally unwilling. But that initial discussion can be crucial for the success of the project. The same here.

The Questions To Ask

But what can you do to increase the chances of success?

You need to be prepared to ask a small number of pertinent questions. But, above all, you have to be prepared to work things out for yourself. In most roles it is impossible to be trained for every eventuality you may encounter. You need to use plenty of initiative. The more you figure things out for yourself, the more useful and successful an employee you will be.

But you will have a small window – a bit like the scoping stage in project management that we discussed earlier – to elicit as much information as you can.

So here are my questions for effective delegation:
- Where can I find out more about the client and this particular job?
- What will my work be used for?
- How long should it take me?
- What are the tricky bits?
- What is the deadline?
- When can I see you next just to make sure I'm on track?
- If you're not around is there anyone else I can talk to?

The way in which delegation is carried out falls on a spectrum. At one end, it's an asking / coaching style, at the other, a telling / directing style.

Delegation is far easier to do in a telling / directing way. Your supervisor simply tells you what to do. But this has less developmental benefit than an asking /

coaching style where your supervisor – by asking questions – gets you to focus on how you will address the task, where you think the challenges will lie and so on.

This is more effective but takes a lot longer while telling / directing is less time-consuming.

If you develop a good relationship with your supervisor you can both agree when they should use one or the other. For instance, in an emergency, they simply tell you what to do. When the time frame is less demanding, they can use an asking / coaching style instead.

The Benefits Of Delegation

Once you are a supervisor you will be faced with this issue: that it takes longer to delegate than do the job yourself. But Stephen Covey, in his book *Seven Habits Of Highly Effective People*, actively encourages delegation. He says it takes more time initially to train someone up to do a job, correcting their mistakes, giving them a chance to try again on a different task, and so on. But it saves considerably more time in the longer run.

A job that a supervisor can do in an hour but will take them three hours to delegate and supervise properly may be one they are tempted to do themselves. But if they do delegate, they are saving time after the third recurrence of that particular task.

The best managers keep their desk under control by delegating. This allows them to spend time on developing people (by delegating then managing by walking about, supporting those they have delegated to) and being available to deal with crises and clients.

This is the sort of supervisor you should aspire to being. Study the styles of those from whom you receive work and see which style is most effective. Then, when you are supervising, see if you can adopt that style.

What Not To Do

Three things you should avoid.

The first is 'upwards delegation'. This is giving the work back to your boss for them to do themselves or to find someone else to do it.

The second is complaining that you haven't received adequate training instead of figuring things out for yourself. Even these days much training is 'on the job' – learning by doing.

The third is asking too many questions. Don't keep on going back with a barrage of questions. Learn which you really need to ask and which you can figure out yourself, then aim to ask them all in one go at the outset.

One of the skills you develop as a young professional is managing and prioritising your workload. If you are any good you will soon receive more work than you can easily do. But it's no good expecting your boss to sort it out with the others who are delegating to you. You need to develop the skills to manage deadlines. But be careful. If you seem too unhelpful you won't receive any work at all. You won't be developing your skills. You won't be useful. You won't be promoted. And your career will stall.

Feedback

The other thing you want – once you've done the job – is feedback on how you have done. I've said earlier that feedback isn't being told how great you are. It's being told where and how you can improve.

If professionals are bad at delegation, they are even worse at feedback. No one likes to criticise a colleague. So you must make it easy for them.

In my view the most effective feedback is immediate and on-the-job. It may be no more than one or two sentences at a time: being told why this was good (so you can repeat it) and how you can do that better. If you are receiving constant little steers as you do a job, it all remains low-key and positive.

If you're not getting regular feedback from your manager you may need to prepare the ground by asking them to fix a time convenient to them while explaining that you're not expecting a discussion of more than 5-10 minutes.

Be prepared to help them provide feedback by having two or three areas or topics you want feedback on (for instance, structure of output, depth of research, etc).

Accept Any Criticism

Whatever you do, don't try to argue against the feedback or justify what you did – this is about learning for the future.

In a slightly different context, whenever I write a book (like this) it is always edited by my long-standing editor who has edited all my books. In the beginning I used to justify what I had written, saying to my editor that she hadn't understood and what I had meant was this not that. But I soon stopped. The whole point of an editor is to make the book better and to make me look a better writer than I am. So now I do whatever my editor says. So, in your case, your supervisor's feedback will make you a better and more successful professional. Don't resist it.

If you make the process easy and enjoyable for your supervisor they are more likely to do it again. But don't ask too often: it can be annoying and smack of lack of self-confidence. Ideally you should get feedback after any piece of work. And if you turn it into a light and brief exchange it will become part of the process.

Models For Feedback

Just so you know, there are several accepted models for the giving of feedback. Here are two.

BOOST stands for Balanced, Objective, Observed, Specific and Timely:

- *Balanced* means setting the bad in the context of the good – sometimes called a praise sandwich (good / bad / good).
- *Objective* means that feedback should be on behaviour, not personality. There's no point in criticising someone because of who they are. It's what they do that feedback is meant to try to change.
- *Observed* means that comments should be based on behaviour that has actually been observed, not on hearsay.
- *Specific* means that comments aren't general and vague but tied directly to the actual work done.
- *Timely* means that it is done as soon after the behaviour in question as possible.

NITA feedback (NITA stands for the National Institute of Trial Advocacy, the body in the US that trains lawyers in courtroom skills) is more directive and, in some respects, easier to apply. There are four stages: Headline, Replay, Rationale and Prescription:

- *Headline* – the person is told what it is about: 'Simon, I'd like to talk to you about your presentation skills.'
- *Replay* – the person is told precisely (as if being played back on video) the behaviour that is being commented on: 'This morning, when you were presenting at the client seminar, you jangled the keys in your trouser pocket all the way through.'
- *Rationale* – the person is given the explanation: 'The trouble with this is that it distracted the audience from the very useful and interesting points that you were making, so they learnt less and came away with an impaired impression of the true level of your expertise.'
- *Prescription* – the person is advised what to do in future: 'Next time, try taking keys and coins out of your pockets so that if you have to put your hands in your pockets there won't be anything in them to jangle.'

The best supervisors use these and other models to give positive as well as negative feedback.

Feedback should be given reasonably regularly – it may just be a few words in the lift or on the way back from a client meeting.

Everyone likes to be praised but it helps to know exactly what you have done right, so you can replicate it, rather than being told in general terms that you were 'fine' or 'really good'.

A Good Feedback Question To Ask

If that's what you've been told – you were 'fine' or 'really good' – ask them what they had to change before acting on your work or sending it to the client.

Sometimes the changes may be stylistic. But being taken through a piece of work you have done and being shown where changes were made and why is always instructive (as my editor does with me).

Two possible issues: your supervisor may not have time, so don't be too demanding; and they may not be able to articulate why they changed what they did. At this level of detail many changes are instinctive, based on many years of experience, and it can often be challenging to explain fully the underlying reasons. So be patient. Ask if you can take the mark-up away to study it for yourself.

If they still seem happy with everything, ask: 'If there was one single thing I could improve, what would it be?'

Appraisal

As you move up the organisation you will receive regular appraisals from your supervisor or line manager (as you become more senior in an organisation you don't have a day-to-day supervisor but a line manager to whom you report on what you're doing from time to time). Unlike feedback, **appraisal** tends to be more formal and may only occur once a year.

One problem with appraisals is that they often occur too far away from the aspects of performance that are being appraised. Effective feedback at frequent intervals overcomes this issue and supports the appraisal process. If you have been seeking feedback on a regular basis, the appraisal should hold no fears and certainly not be the place where you learn of 'do-betters' for the first time.

However, in many organisations appraisals are either done poorly or not at all. Most supervisors hate giving appraisals because of the implication that they are required to be critical. Again, make their task easy: it's your job to get an effective appraisal so that you know where and how you can improve your performance. Only by doing that will you increase your prospects. Be a willing appraisee.

One way of doing this is to help make the appraisal into a forward-looking process rather than something that is looking backwards at the previous year.

Ask your supervisor what the department or team's plans for the next year are and how you can play your part in helping meet those objectives. This is a good way of showing enthusiasm and of being able to discuss what sort of work you want to receive. By offering you are more likely to get some of what you want. But you also need to explore with your supervisor where you need to improve your skills in order to take on the work that you would like.

Cast in this more positive, forward-looking light, the appraisal becomes more of a discussion. Your supervisor is more likely to relax and give you an honest assessment of the areas on which you need to work. You can then ask for development opportunities and / or training to be able to develop those skills. And you can be sure that what you are doing is in line with the team or department's plans so you are more likely to be doing what your boss wants.

Of course, there may come a time when your appraisals seem negative. Don't take it personally. It may simply be time for you to move on to another organisation where your skills fit more readily with their strategy. In short, don't be afraid of appraisals: far better to know what people really think of you than to be kept in the dark and to be unaware of views being expressed behind your back. Ultimately your goal is to be a successful professional. And you can only do that in an organisation where your skills fit. So you owe it to yourself to be sure that they do. If you are in an organisation where appraisals are done badly or not at all and you aren't getting any encouragement or decent responses to questions about the team's plans, you may be in the wrong place.

Time Management

I mentioned earlier that as a junior professional, you will find there are many demands on your time and you need to start prioritising. Books on time management (if you can find the time to read them) tend to cover three things, which I label: Head, Desk, Door. How you manage time depends on what is in your head, what is on your desk and what (and who) comes in through the door.

What's in your head This is about how you work, what your working patterns are and what your aims are. It reflects how you are as a person. It includes: how you prioritise (different types of To Do list), decision-making models, creative thinking, breaking jobs into chunks (for instance, read the information the night before to let the brain pickle the issues overnight), your peak working time (biorhythms), physical exercise and stress management.

It's also about how to set goals and how to reduce the time you spend on jobs (for instance, always set deadlines otherwise the task expands to fill the available time) and how to maximise the benefit of the time you do spend.

What's on your desk This is about the actual work you have on your desk: how you manage it and how you do it. This is where most of the tips come in. They're basically about reading, writing, communicating and binning. For instance: never pick up a piece of paper more than once without actioning it; always use the bin in preference to any other type of file; when to use email and how to use it; how to read (reduce the volume you read and only skim read what you keep); making appointments with yourself; and so on.

What comes in through the door This is about controlling the incoming flow of work and learning how to deal with others. Keep a timesheet of what – and who – fills the day. Analyse interruptions and reduce them.

In the case of work, should you be doing it? To answer this you need to understand the value of your function in the eyes of the organisation and what you should and should not be doing if they are to get the best out of you. In your early days you will do whatever you are given. But as you become more senior there will be opportunities for ensuring you get the work you should – for instance through the appraisal process.

A receptionist at a place where I worked found that she was being dumped on: all sorts of stuff was being given to her to do as people came in or left the building (usually in a hurry). She would always do the task, then when they returned or passed her desk again she would, in the politest way, explain a better way of getting the task done (better for them, and usually involving someone else) so that she didn't get dumped on again.

This had two effects. She got to know the people in the organisation really well. And they came to really value her. In time they wouldn't dump something on her. They'd ask her how best to get it done.

Her role had changed from 'doer' to 'adviser' – which of course allowed her to get on with her proper job of being a receptionist. In time she moved into a different role, having demonstrated her worth.

Working With Others

You are likely to find yourself working as part of a team. As the world becomes more complex, tasks can no longer be entrusted to one person to carry out.

Instead work is increasingly team-based with different members bringing their own expertise to bear on the project. Crucial to a project's success is the way the team itself functions.

Many assessment centres include an exercise in which applicants for a role have to work together.

There is a balance to be struck between being too domineering – speaking more than others and crowding them out – and saying nothing at all.

You need to work out why you are there: what is the purpose of this particular team and what is your role in it?

In an assessment centre the purpose of the team may be to come up with solutions to a particular issue. So you need to do two things: suggest possible solutions; and critique those suggested by others.

Working In Teams

What matters here is quality not quantity: one good idea rather than three that obviously won't work. And critiquing means building on others' suggestions rather than shooting them down. So the key is to be constructive, positive and participative. If you make a few good suggestions and each is seized on by others then you will be valued and remembered.

Over time as you gain experience of working in teams you will see that people play particular roles. Some are good at coming up with ideas. Others are good at organising people and tasks. Others keep an eye on the clock and make sure the team works towards the deadline. Others are doers and get things done. Others know who outside the team may be able to help, and so on.

Try to work out what your preferred role is and what else you may need to do to ensure the team is properly functioning. As with project management debriefs, it is worthwhile to encourage the team to look at its own processes, see how it got tasks done and identify where it could improve.

All of this is about building an awareness of yourself and others and the roles you play in a team and an organisation. This is all part of what I believe to be the 'awareness' of 'commercial awareness'.

This is just the start of building your career. Let's see what else you need to consider.

CHAPTER 11

BUILDING YOUR BRAND

Managing client expectations – client satisfaction – complaints about price – failures in service quality – Parasuraman Quality Gap Model – relating to real clients – analyticals, leaders and visionaries – open and closed questions – contextualise your advice – networking – referrals on a conflict – multipliers – developing your career – David Maister's 'How's Your Asset?' – leadership

You are now embarked on your career. Sooner or later you will start dealing with real clients. Managing client expectations is perhaps the single most important aspect to being a successful professional.

Managing Client Expectations

Try this. A client rings up. They need a document in a hurry. You ask when. They say tomorrow by midday. It's going to be a stretch for you to do it. Reluctantly you agree. Next day you manage to get the document finished but later than you had hoped. You've still done an amazing job to get it out – you had to work till midnight the night before. But the client still only gets it mid-afternoon at 3.30. The client is disappointed – because you over-promised and under-delivered.

Now try this. A client rings up. They need a document in a hurry. You ask when. They say tomorrow by midday. You ask why. They say they need it to put in a pack which will go to the board of directors. When is it going, you ask. First thing the day after tomorrow, which is why they need to have everything ready by end of business tomorrow which is why they said midday. You ask a bit more about the form of document. They say it has to be short, no more than a page (that's good, you think, you were going to write 10 pages).

You promise them they will have it no later than 5pm tomorrow in the format they wanted. You do the job (without having to stay late, because it's shorter than you would have made it if you hadn't asked) and get it round to them by 3.30 the next day. They are delighted. You have under-promised and over-delivered.

In each case you got it to them at the same time. But in the second, most importantly, you have earned their trust as somebody who not only meets his or her promise but exceeds it. So next time they will be a bit more relaxed and give you a more realistic deadline – without your having to negotiate it.

What matters isn't what actually happens. It's what *actually happens* set against what the client *expected to happen*. You can still do the same thing and deliver it at the same time but how the client reacts has nothing to do with that, but with what you led the client to expect.

Client Satisfaction Is Relative

In other words, client satisfaction is a relative, not an absolute, and it depends on the client's *perception* of what was actually delivered against the client's *expectation* of what should have been delivered.

Professionals who are good with clients grasp this: they probe the client's concerns; they get to the bottom of deadlines. They make their own lives easier as a result, impress the client each time and create terrific client relations. All of this builds up a bank of trust so that when something does go genuinely wrong, the client is more forgiving.

But what happens when something goes wrong? What matters here is rebuilding trust.

Rebuilding Trust

If you get an angry client on the phone, try the following.

Apologise – say you are sorry that they are having this trouble (even if the client is in the wrong, what you are apologising for is the fact they are upset).

Empathise – try to feel what it is they are feeling and try to show that you share their point of view.

Don't blame other parts of your organisation – it never sounds good when someone in a service organisation blames another part of it or another colleague.

Start to rebuild trust – make a promise you can keep. Don't promise to look into it and get back to them – because if you are unable to find anything out immediately you might not feel you can call them until you do, which may be a day or two later. Instead, tell them you will see what you can find out and will call at a certain time later that day. Then make sure you do so, even if you have nothing to report – that way you start to rebuild trust.

Make sure you take a full note of the complaint and say you will investigate.

Tell your supervisor – and tell the client you have done so.

Complaints About Price

Clients find it difficult to express concerns about service – for two reasons. Service is intangible. It's not a thing, it's a feeling. You know when you're getting good service and bad but it's often difficult to express. And, second, if you can express it, you are implicitly criticising whoever provided the service. Clients don't like criticising professionals who work with them. It can sour the relationship.

So often they say nothing. Or, if they say anything, it may be about the price of the job – what they have been charged. Price is complex, as we saw previously. And professionals are poor at explaining price in terms of the value the client derives from the work done.

So if a client complains about price be aware that there may be a lot going on beneath the surface of the complaint. It may actually be a complaint about service. The client didn't feel they were getting the service they paid for. You need to probe very gently to find out what is really bugging them.

Equally, a client complaint can often be the start of an even deeper and better client relationship. Clients are often embarrassed to complain. If you make it easy for them and resolve the issue they will often feel a sense of gratitude that is out of proportion to the benefit you've provided. They will feel it's all right to tell you what they think and they will like you even more because they feel able to do so.

Failures In Service Quality

This is such a big issue in client relationships that a team of researchers led by an academic called Parasuraman devised the **Parasuraman Quality Gap Model**.

What the model addresses is where misunderstandings can occur between what the client expects and what the organisation actually delivers. At each stage in the process there can be a slip – however slight – between what someone is told (or understands) and what is actually done. So, for example:

- The client wants something done (*expectation*)
- The person the client talks to hears slightly differently what the client wants
- They pass the client's instruction down the client team but it is subtly changed in the telling
- What the team actually do is a bit different from what the team were told
- What the team tell the team leader they have done is a bit different from what they have actually done
- What the team leader tells the client has been done is different from what the team leader was told and has actually been done
- Finally, what the client hears the organisation has done (*perception*) is a bit different from what the team leader said

Any of these will mean the result is different from the client's original expectation. Result: dissatisfaction.

Set out like this it can actually make you wonder how any sort of client service is provided at all to a client's satisfaction. The mismatch at any stage can be slight but lead to a wide gap between expectation and perception.

Once you identify the stage at which a 'gap' occurred – for instance through a project debrief with the client – you can then guard against making the same mistake next time.

If There's One Thing…

Do you remember that question I suggested you ask when you get great feedback – 'If there was one single thing I could improve, what would it be?'

You can also use it with clients.

A colleague of mine once put this question to a client in a project debrief. The client had been effusive in their praise of the project with no criticism at all. Finally, my colleague said to the client: 'That's all great. But if there was one single thing we could improve, what would it be?'

The client said – and this was (if you can believe it) before email, devices and texting – that they had had trouble getting through to my colleague and the team after 5pm because that's when our switchboard closed.

My colleague immediately went to the relevant person in the organisation and evening cover for the switchboard was arranged so that all clients could get through to us out of office hours.

A Lesson In Client Service

This story illustrates another point about client service. Professionals obsess with the quality of their technical advice. Clients don't. They take technical quality as a given. That's why they have come to your organisation. Unless they too, are experts, they won't be able to tell how good the advice is.

But what they do care about is client service: basic things such as how soon their phone calls are returned; how practical and helpful the advice is; how well-written the communications are (whether the language used is accurate or contains typos); whether you are punctual; whether you do what you say you will. None of these things is technically demanding.

But you'd be surprised at how poor professionals are when it comes to service quality. In truth clients will judge the quality of the technical work by the quality of the service. If you are late or your emails are full of typos, the client may not think you know what you're talking about.

So, getting the switchboard open in the evening – which had nothing to do with our technical expertise – mattered as much, if not more so, to the client than our technical advice.

Of course, if you ask the question ('If there was one single thing we could improve, what would it be?') you absolutely have to be able to act upon the answer, whatever it is. Otherwise you are raising expectations and then failing to meet them, leaving the client more dissatisfied than if you hadn't asked the question at all.

Relating To Real Clients

If you are going to make the best impression with a new client – your boss included – you need to make a quick assessment of the sort of person they are.

As you can imagine there is a lot of theory around about how to do this. The trouble with much of this theory is that it is at best superficial, people being the complicated creatures they are. I dislike attempts to put people into boxes. But these models help you think in advance about the sort of person you are about to meet, which is their real value.

Based on work by (amongst others) David Merrill and Tony Reiss, I tend to think of people in the workplace as falling into three types.

Analyticals, Leaders And Visionaries

Many professionals are 'analytical'. They tend to be task-focused. They ask questions and want lots of detail. Your supervisor may well be analytical, so always go prepared (always have paper and pen with you to write down what they need you to find out). You need to think through all of the possible options because analyticals will grill you extensively with close and detailed questioning. Prepare your case in advance – attend to detail, be clear, and avoid emotional argument. They are often poor at issuing direct instructions. You may have to tease out of them what exactly they want you to do.

By contrast, many business people – clients – are either 'leaders' or 'visionaries'. Leaders are also task-oriented, but they tend to issue orders rather than ask questions. They are action-oriented. They want options and solutions, succinctly expressed. So, with them, be brief and to the point. Stick to business and skip the chit-chat. Persuade them by citing objectives and results. Senior people in large corporates are like this.

Visionaries also get bored by detail but like enthusiasm and energy. They want to know what the effect of something will be and they drive things along through sheer personality. So, with them you need to be lively, to entertain and to stimulate. Ask them for their opinions. Keep your eye on the big picture and don't drown them in technical detail. Many entrepreneurs are like this.

Leaders and visionaries are very different from analytical types and analyticals often don't get on very well with them. Business leaders and visionaries understand why professionals are important and why they need to consult them. But they don't often like them.

The professionals who are best at building client relationships understand this and dial back the professional fussiness and attention-to-detail (they do all of that in the background) and when they are with clients try to relate to them as leaders and visionaries.

Now, the purpose of this model is not to enable you to make superficial judgements about others. What it actually does is to make you think what other people might be like in advance of meeting and working with them, and to factor this into your thoughts and actions.

The aim is to start to build a personal relationship. You don't have to become their friends exactly. Some clients don't want that. They have no small talk and have no interest in you. And any attempt by you to find out about them may risk being seen as intrusive and inappropriate.

If you are going to make the best impression with a new client you need to get on their wavelength. One way of doing that is by asking them about their business and their role in it. People in business tend to like to talk about it. It excites them. It's why they get out of bed in the morning. So asking them about their business and their role in it is a good way in. This is where commercial awareness comes in. Your knowledge of business and their organisation will enable you to sustain a conversation.

Professionals start off with one huge disadvantage. We think of ourselves as experts who give advice. And that means we think we only give value when we are imparting advice or information. And that means we talk.

Think of the last date you went on. Who do you think enjoyed it the most? You or your date? Then ask yourself: who did most of the talking?

When we talk we tend to enjoy ourselves. When someone is talking at us all the time we get bored and frustrated.

Ask Questions

So the key to getting off on the right foot with a client is to listen and ask questions. It's a cliché but you have two ears and one mouth: use them in that proportion.

In professional life you want to be *interested* rather than *interesting*. So ask questions rather than talk at people. In particular, ask open questions.

An **open question** is one which begins with a word like How or What or Why or Where or When. It is 'open' because it allows the other person to fashion a reply in whatever style and to whatever length they like. It opens them up.

A **closed question** is a direct question implying a yes or no answer. 'Do you feel OK?' is a closed question. 'How are you feeling?' is an open question. Closed questions are necessary sometimes, for instance to check your own understanding of what someone has said (for instance when being delegated to).

Open questions are good when starting to get to know people.

One of the great secrets of professional life which never seems to be mentioned anywhere is that at its heart it is about meeting and dealing with people. Not all clients want to be friendly. They often have too many other things going on.

But if you show them – using some of the techniques mentioned here – that you are good at getting their work done and responsive to their needs, they will like you and you can get to know them.

And the more you get to know a client the easier your job is because you will learn the pressures they are under and what works best for them. And then if things go wrong they will be more forgiving.

And the funny thing about business is that clients don't value the professionals who know the most or who are the most expert; they value those advisers who enable them to get to where they want their business to be.

Contextualise Your Advice

The more you understand what your client is trying to do and where the advice you give fits into that picture, the more you will be providing advice and assistance that your client really appreciates. In other words, you will contextualise your advice so it fits with what the client is trying to do. The sorts of internal question that can help you do this include:

- What is prompting my client to ask me for this help?
- What are my client's aims and goals – generally and in relation to this in particular?
- How will what I do help my client achieve those goals?
- How is my client going to use or act on my advice?
- How best can I present this advice for my client to use most effectively?
- How can I check all along the way that what I am doing is what my client wants?
- What should I do by way of follow-up once I have completed doing what my client has asked me to?

These questions will help you tailor what you do to make it relevant to what the client wants. You don't have to be the most brilliant person in your year to be a hero to your clients. Usually the professionals with the best client skills aren't the most brainy or learned of advisers. And anyone can develop these skills.

Networking

So far we have been looking in detail at the anatomy of client-professional relationships. But professionals have to do more than look after existing clients. They have to find new ones. The way they do this is through networking. It's only if a prospective client has heard of you that they will invite you to pitch. So networking is about meeting other people and getting to know them.

The problem is that networking has been taken as a short-hand for 'getting business'. As a student or young professional, you may well have been encouraged to think that 'networking' is about getting the contact details of senior people so you can then ask them for a job. All of this makes networking seem selfish: it's about me. Actually, the best networkers think the opposite. They make it about the other person.

Finding Like-Minded People

In one sense we've been networking all our lives. At school you find like-minded people whose company you enjoy. They become your network. The same is true in professional life. You look for people with similar interests and outlooks who may in time become friends. Almost all my friends have come through work.

Your first network as a professional will be other people who do the same thing as you. Professionals bond best with others who do the same job. We share similar outlooks, challenges and frustrations. These are also likely to be your competitors if they do the same sort of work for rival employers. This is fine.

A professional once asked me how he could develop a reputation for his expertise. I asked him about his relations with other professionals in his field in other, competitor organisations. He was hostile towards them, he said, because they were competitors.

I said I thought this was a mistake. He probably had more in common with them – given that they did the same thing – than he thought. 'Besides,' I said, 'when a client wants to know if anyone is any good, who does he ask?'

'Other professionals,' he said.

'Exactly. That's why you need to know them and they you. Unless your competitors think well of you, how can you expect potential clients to?'

This is why it's good to get on with competitors.

Referrals On A Conflict

If for some reason a professional cannot act for a client because of, say, a conflict of interest (their organisation acts for the client's competitor) they will want to refer that client to someone who is a 'safe pair of hands' – who will do the job and still give the client back to them. If they think you're good and they like and trust you, you may well get that referral.

It's also surprising how many competitors go on to other jobs (for instance, going in-house) in which they can become your potential clients.

Besides, one thing that irritates clients enormously is having professional advisers who don't get on with each other but waste time by point scoring, jockeying for position and trying to out-compete each other.

Some of your best contacts will be what are known as **multipliers**. They may not be in a position to give you work themselves but they can influence others who can. These opinion formers are important. In the example above, the professional's competitors were multipliers. They wouldn't give him any work directly (except, say, on a conflict) but they could influence potential clients who might.

Who To Network With

So, as I say, networking is not about finding other people who can help your career. It's about finding other people with whom you have things in common. If they become good contacts they will inevitably help you in your career if they like you and are able to. The point of networking, then, is not to find people who can help you but to find people you can help.

If you try to make contacts because it's good for your career, other people will smell your insincerity. It'll show because they will detect that you are more interested in yourself than in them.

Unplanned Benefits

The problem is you can't plan any of this, because you never know where work and clients are going to come from. A wise professional told me that he spent part of his career in Asia and when he returned to London he had to build his client base from scratch. So over a six-month period he looked up everyone he knew and explained he was back and specified the things he thought he could do best.

'Within weeks I was hit by a wall of work,' he said, 'but in each case it wasn't clear to me where the work had come from. Someone I knew must have mentioned my name to someone who didn't, and so on. So I couldn't trace a line between talking to this person and getting that client or that piece of work. The only thing I know for sure is that if I hadn't bothered to get in touch with all of my contacts I would have got no work at all.'

The important thing is that he didn't get in touch with his contacts asking them for work. He simply wanted to tell them that he was back and what he was up to and what he was looking for.

Networking – An Example

A colleague of mine was a property lawyer. He was very commercial. He loved the property market and talking to people in it. He liked introducing clients to each other so they could do deals. Clients loved him – he knew so much about the property market – and gave him a lot of work.

One day he came into the office from vacation. I asked him where he had been. 'Australia,' he said. I asked him what it was like but he didn't tell me. Instead he talked about someone he'd met in the hotel bar. He knew nothing about this man but they had had a very interesting conversation about the London property market. When eventually they swapped contact details it turned out this man was the chief investment officer for a major Australian pension fund. A few months later the pension fund decided to invest massively in the London commercial property market and needed a lawyer. Guess who got the job?

Of course, networking is also a terrific way of increasing your commercial awareness. When people in business get together they talk about work. Networking is an excellent opportunity to find out about different sectors from people who work in them.

As you get to know people in a client organisation, ask them about their area and the particular challenges they face.

Doing these things will enhance your understanding of what your clients are doing and why, and the issues they encounter. You will be able to engage them in interesting conversations which will increase your understanding of them and their respect for you.

Developing Your Career

'How's Your Asset?' – an article by David Maister which is also in his book *Managing The Professional Service Firm* – is a wonderful reminder to all professionals that from time to time they need to look up from what is on their desk to make sure they develop skills that will remain relevant to the market place for the future.

Maister's point is that professional work is demanding, stressful and takes up all of your time. But it may not in itself ensure you are developing in the way you want or need to if you are to remain in demand amongst clients.

Every so often you have to look up from the desk and ask yourself how your asset is, meaning your expertise, know-how and brand.

In a sense it's about having a personal strategy and knowing in which direction you want your expertise to develop. Maister is warning us that we need to check from time to time that our personal strategic direction is still relevant to the market in which we work.

Doing this will help you become a 'reflective professional'. A bit like Maister, the idea here is that you keep what you are doing and how you do it under regular review. It's like doing a project management debrief but just for you. The purpose is to help you improve. It can form part of a learning log or the notes you keep in connection with your regular appraisals.

How To Be A Leader

In due course, as you progress in your career you will be leading others. You might think it a bit premature to be thinking about leadership (if you don't then it is). After all, isn't **leadership** what the people at the top of organisations need to demonstrate and worry about?

Not so. As soon as you start managing one or more other people you are effectively a leader and this will happen much sooner in your professional life than you might expect.

There is an awful lot written about leadership – almost as much as there is on strategy. There are leadership skills that can be developed and learnt. The idea that a leader is born not made is out of date as is the stereotype of a leader as someone who is charismatic and commanding. Neither is true.

One of the best books is *Why Should Anyone Be Led By You?* by Rob Goffee and Gareth Jones. I used this when I became the leader of a large team. It focused on four aspects of leadership which I reorganised into an acronym that spells ACES. The four are: Authenticity, Community, Excitement and Significance.

Authenticity is about showing who you really are, including your weaknesses. It's a mistake for a leader to think he or she needs to be all-knowing and always right. Team members want to be useful. They want the leader to rely on them and seek their input. If you know your weaknesses and are not afraid to show them you can get your team to fill in your gaps.

Community is about fostering a sense of togetherness. The best teams like each other, respect each other and like working together. Doing things together outside work often helps. Knowing what people do outside work and allowing them to bring that experience into the workplace also helps.

Excitement is about making the work interesting. The most humdrum jobs can be made exciting if people feel they can contribute to how the work is done and how processes can be improved.

Significance is about helping team members feel that what they do at work is worthwhile. It should be, because otherwise the role wouldn't exist. But the best leaders help their teams learn and develop so that in time they can go on to bigger and better things.

Doesn't that sound like a team you'd like to work in?

As you rise up through the organisation, study the organisation's most effective leaders and what they do, so that in time you can become one too.

CHAPTER 12

WHAT IS COMMERCIAL AWARENESS?

The single most compelling reason for being commercially aware

So what is commercial awareness? You should have an idea by now. Your view may not be the same as mine but that's OK because there isn't a single right answer.

My answer is that it's everything.

It's all around you. It's in how we live, what we need, the work we do, the economics of our way of life.

So, to the question 'What is commercial awareness?' I answer: it's a mindset.

It's not something you can magically get or buy or fake. You can't switch it on for an interview then switch it back off again.

It's an attitude of mind. It's an interest in the commercial world around you – which you, with luck, will soon be a part of.

For a lot of business people it's what gives life meaning.

We've been on quite a journey. We've looked at what business is about (innovation), the importance of customers, strategy and business development. We've looked at the role of money and the difference between cash flow and profit. We've looked how businesses are organised internally and how they interact with professional service firms that serve them (which are businesses themselves). We've looked at clients as organisations but also as individuals and how your first client will be your supervisor.

We've seen how this fits with the term 'commercial awareness'. The 'commercial' bit is understanding business. The 'awareness' is about serving clients as individuals, being aware of what they need from you.

I hope to have got you interested in business. Its effects and benefits are all around us. And I hope that once you have that interest and enthusiasm, it never leaves you. If so, it means you have the mindset. You are commercially aware.

My mother used to read the business pages every day, well into old age. Even then she used to say to me: 'I can't walk past a shop without wondering what its turnover is.'

I once worked as the editor of magazines about law and finance which were read by people who worked in large financial institutions.

The boss of the company was my line manager and he had no small talk whatsoever. He was only interested in business – and he asked the weirdest questions.

We might be in a taxi going to a business meeting. We might stop at a traffic light and a cyclist would draw up alongside. 'Are more people cycling to work?' he'd ask me. Or there might be a showroom full of showers you could install in your bathroom and he'd ask: 'Are more people taking showers than baths these days?'

I had no answers and, even worse, no idea why he was asking these bizarre questions.

Then one day I understood. If more people were cycling to work and fewer people taking trains or buses, then there were fewer opportunities for people to read our publications. The same with showers. You can't read a magazine in a shower. You can (if you're so inclined) in a bath.

The point wasn't the actual questions he was asking. It was the fact he was asking questions at all. He was constantly looking ahead at the way people lived and how it might affect our business. It's what the best business leaders do. They are asking all the time why we do things in a certain way and how things are changing.

This is the single most compelling reason for being commercially aware. The best business people (the sort of people you want to work for and have as clients) are switched on, interesting, interested people. They are helping to change the world – before it changes them.

I find business exciting and the people who work in it interesting. I know most of what I know about business from talking to people, engaging them in discussions and asking questions.

In my experience, busy professionals are very generous with their time when helping young people with career choices. But don't waste those opportunities. Be well informed. Ask good questions. Don't pretend to know when you don't. Don't try to fake it. You need to know enough to ask good questions and understand the answers, which in turn will lead to more good questions and a genuine discussion. And a few of these people you talk to will become mentors and friends.

If you develop this mindset you will feel the excitement of the world around you. It will make your life richer and more interesting.

If you are genuinely committed and have the right attitude, it will show. This, to my mind, is what employers are looking for.

Good luck in your future career – and I hope this book helps you to achieve all your goals.

FURTHER READING

If you have set your heart on a career in the financial world, you might like my book *All You Need To Know About The City*. I believe that anyone working in business has to have some understanding of the financial markets. Generations of students and young professionals have told me they've found this book helpful.

I haven't talked here about the need to write clearly and succinctly in business. But it is a crucial business skill. How well you communicate at work will be integral to your success. My book *Get To The Point* is about writing effectively in the workplace and contains the tips you need to make the change from writing for academic studies to writing for business clients.

If you are thinking of becoming a lawyer then you could try my book *Is Law For You?* which gives an overview of what the law is and explains what being a lawyer is really like.

INDEX / GLOSSARY

A

Account managers 66
Accountants 64
Acquisition finance 47
Actuaries 65
Advertising 14
Alternative fee structures 87
Amortisation 44
Analyticals 122
Antitrust 55
Appraisal 60, 63, 113
Architects 68
Asset finance 46, 55
Associates 70
Audit 48, 64
Auditors 48, 64

B

Back office 63
Balance of payments 55
Balance sheet 38
Balanced scorecard 50
Bankers 65
Barriers to entry 23
Best practice 25
Best-in-class 25, 63
Bidder 35
Board of directors 60
BOOST 112
Boston Consulting Group 21, 97
BCG Product or Growth
    Share Matrix 21
Brand 13, 41
Brand extension 14
Brand management 14, 61
Bricks 'n' clicks 23
Brokers 65

Bullet 47
Business development (BD) 13, 61
Business Process Re-engineering
    (BPR) 25
Business schools 60
Business to Business (B2B) 11
Business to Consumer (B2C) 11
Buyers 21

C

Capitalist economies 52
Cartels 55
Cash conversion 49
Cash flow 31-33
Cash flow statement 45
Central banks 57
Chairman 60
Channels to market 14, 23
Charge 30, 47
Chargeable time 72
Chief Executive Officer (CEO) 60
Chief Financial Officer (CFO) 61
Chief Information Officer (CIO) ... 24, 62
Chief Operating Officer (COO) 60
Client expectations 118
Client Relationship Management
    (CRM) 74
Client satisfaction 118
Closed question 123
Comfort letter 47
Commercial bank 30
Commercialisation 54
Commoditisation 73
Communist economies 52
Competition authority 55
Competition law 35
Competitive tender 78

Competitors 21
Complaints 119
Concession 54
Conditional sale 46
Consolidation 35
Consumer durables 13
Consumer research 14
Consumerism 23
Consumers 11
Contextualised advice 124
Continuous improvement 25, 62
Convergence of content 22
Convergence of platforms 22
Copyright 24, 62
Copywriters 66
Copywriting 14
Core 25
Corporate 29
Corporates 8
Corporate finance 64
Corporate identity 14, 61
Corporate governance 58
Corporate responsibility 58
Cost centres 63
Creditors 48
Culture 19, 76, 106
Currency swap 48
Current assets 39
Customer segmentation 14
Customer value management 15
Customers 11

D
Data mining 15
Data warehouses 15
David Maister 73-76, 127
Debenture 47
Debrief 95
Debtors 48
Defaults 47
Deflation 57

Delegation 108
Demand 56
Depreciation 43
Derivatives 47
Differentiate 13
Digital agencies 14, 66
Disintermediation 23
Disruptive technology 23
Diversification 35
Dividends 31
Dominant market positions 36, 55

E
Ebitda 45
Economies of scale 31
Enforce its security 47
Engineers 68
Enterprise Resource Planning
  (ERP) 25, 63, 68
Entrepreneurs 10
Equities 29
Equity 29
Equity partners 70
Expenses 72

F
Facilities Management 63
Factoring 46
Fast-Moving Consumer Goods
  (FMCGs) 13
Fee-earners 70
Feedback 104, 111
Finance Director (FD) 61
Finance leasing 46, 55
Fixed 47
Fixed assets 39
Fixed costs 41
Fixed price 86
Floating 35, 47
Forward 48
Franchise 33, 34, 54

Functions 60
Fund managers 65
Future 48

G

Gearing 30
Global initial public offering 54
Globalisation 23
Going public 35
Graphic designers 66
Gross Domestic Product (GDP) 55
Gross margin 49
Gross profit 41
Guarantees 47

H

Health & Safety (H&S) 63
Hedging 47
Henry Mintzberg 76
Highly geared 47
Hire purchase 46
Holding company 47
Host company 65
Human Resources 63

I

Income statement 38
Incorporate 28
Inflation 56
In-house lawyers 67
In-house legal function 63
Initial Public Offering (IPO) 35
Innovation 10
Insolvent 28
Institutional investors 48
Insurance 63
Insurance brokers 65
Insureds 65
Intellectual property (IP) 62
Intellectual Property Rights (IPR) . 24, 62
Interest 30
Interest cover 49

Interest-rate swap 48
Interest rates 56
Interim 48
Interior designers 68
Interview 102
Inventory 15
Inventory management 15
Investment bank 36
Investor relations 66
Invitation To Tender (ITT) 78
Invoice discounting 46

J

Joint and several liability 28, 71
Just-in-time production 25, 61

K

Kaizen 25, 61
Key man insurance 66
Key Performance Indicators (KPIs) ... 50
Knowledge economy 24, 62
Knowledge management 24, 62
Knowledge workers 24

L

Lawyers 67
Leaders 122
Leadership 128
Learning & Development 63
Legacy systems 68
Legal departments 67
Legal executives 67
Leverage 30, 49, 72
Leveraged Buy Out (LBO) 47
Levers of Profitability 71
Limited liability partnerships (LLPs) ... 71
Line manager 60, 108
Listing 35
Lobbyists 61, 67
Lock-up 73
Lockstep 70
Logistics 15, 62

Long list 78
Longtail effect 16
Loss adjusters 65
Low-ball 79

M

Management Buy Outs (MBOs) 36
Management consultants 68
Manufacturing economy 62
Marcoms 14
Margins 41
Market capitalisation 25
Market dominant 36, 55
Market liberalisation 54
Market research 66
Marketing 13, 61
Marketing consultants 66
Mass customisation 16
Mass marketing 14
McKinsey 19, 76
Media and advertising agencies 66
Media businesses 14
Media buyers 66
Media buying 14
Mergers & Acquisitions (M&A) 35
Micromarketing 15
Mission 19
Models 20
Monitoring progress 94
Monopolies 36, 54
Moral editing 72
Multinational companies (MNCs) .. 8, 23
Multipliers 125

N

Name recognition 35
Nationalisation 53
Near-shoring 25
Net present value 50
Net profit 41
Network effect 16

Networking 124
New entrants 21
NITA feedback 112
Non-core 25
Non-executive director 60
Non-Governmental Organisations
 (NGOs) 52
Normative strategies 76, 101
Not-for-profits 52

O

Off Balance Sheet (OBS) 54
Offshoring 25
Open question 123
Operating company 47
Operating margin 49
Option 48
Organisational design 64
Outsource 64
Outsourcing 25
Overheads 41

P

Panel 78
Paradigm shifts 23
Paralegals 67
Parasuraman Quality Gap Model 120
Parent company guarantee 47
Pareto Principle 74, 97
Partners 70
Partnership 28, 70
Patent attorneys 67
Patents 24, 62
Personal liability 28
PESTL 22
Peter Drucker 18, 24, 62
Pitch 78
Pitching 78
Plan sponsor 65
Planning 94
Porter's Five Forces 21, 76
Portfolio 62

PR consultants 66
Pre-qualified 79
Press or Public Relations (PR) ... 14, 66
Price/earnings ratio 50
Pricing 85
Principal 30
Private company 29
Private equity 34
Private Finance Initiative (PFI) 54
Private sector 52
Privatisation 53
Process 20
Procurement 62
Product lifecycle 16
Product placement 14
Production 61
Professional service firms
 (PSFs) 8, 24, 64, 68, 69, 77
Profit 28, 44
Profit & Loss (P&L) 38
Profit centre 63
Project creep 93
Project management (PM) 90
Project scope 93
Property consultants 67
Public affairs 61, 67
Public companies 29
Public Private Partnership (PPP) 54
Public relations (PR) 14, 61, 66
Public sector 52
Public Sector Borrowing
 Requirement (PSBR) 56

Q
Quality movement 62
Quantity surveyors 68

R
Rate 72
Real value 56
Receivables 46

Regulation 55
Regulator 54
Remuneration committee 60
Reporting accountants 64
Reputational risk 61, 63
Request For Particulars (RFP) 78
Research & Development (R&D) 62
Retail 11
Retail banking 30
Retail customers 11
Retail sales 11
Retained earnings 39
Return on Capital Employed
 (ROCE) 40, 49
Return on Investment (ROI) 14, 40
Revolver 47
Revolving credit facility 47
Risk management 63
RULES 72
Run on the bank 56

S
Salaried partners 70
Sales 13, 61
Sales force 13
Sales force automation 15
Sales promotion 13, 66
Scenario planning 26
Scope 90, 94-96
Scope creep 90, 93
Secular trends 23
Secured lending 30
Security 47
Selling 13
Senior associate 70
Service economy 62
Service level agreements (SLAs) 64
Servicing debt 30
Short list 78
Small and Medium Size Enterprises
 (SMEs) 29

Software as a Service (SaaS) 23
Sole trader 28
Speed 73
Stakeholders 58
Start-up capital 28
Step changes 23
Stephen Mayson 72, 74, 76, 101
Strategy 18, 97
Structural engineers 68
Substitutes 21
Supervisor 108
Suppliers 21
Supply 56
Supply chain finance 46
Supply chain management 15, 62
SWOT analysis (strengths, weaknesses, opportunities, threats) 20
Syndicated loan 47

T

Takeover 35
Target 35
Tax advisers 64
Teams 116
Term loan 47
Theory of the business 18
Third sector 52
Three Fs 33
Time management 114
Time recording 71
Time to market 16
Trade sale 54
Trade marks 24, 62, 67
Trade-off triangle 96
Trainees 70
Treasury 61
Trophy client 79, 93, 98

U

Unicorns 34
Unique Selling Proposition (USP) 13
Unit cost 31

Unwind 48
Utilisation 72

V

Value For Money (VFM) 85
Variable costs 41
Venture capitalists (VCs) 33
Vision 19
Visionaries 122

W

Wholly-owned subsidiary 35
Work-in-progress (WIP) 73
Working capital 28
Working capital requirement 46, 73